CHARLES MANSON

CHARLES MANSON

The Interviews: Volume 8

ALAN R. WARREN

Copyright

Charles Manson: The Interviews
Written by Alan R. Warren
Published by House of Mystery

Cover design, formatting, layout, and editing by Evening Sky Publishing Services

Published in the United States of America
ISBN (Paperback): 978-1-998680-10-8
ISBN (eBook): 978–1-998680-11-5

Contents

Introduction

Throughout the last fourteen years of conducting interviews for both radio and writing books and articles, one of the most fascinating cases I have encountered was the Charles Manson case. This case had everything. It had several brutal murder scenes, cult-like behavior, celebrities, rock stars, hippies, and drugs. To top things off, ever since the murder trial was over, several conspiracy theories were soon to follow, and they did.

So, what happened? Was Charlie Manson really in control of his Family commune members enough to make them commit all the murders? Did they believe in Helter Skelter, the Beatles? And a race war was about to happen in the late sixties? Along with those questions, now we have writers claiming that Manson was using the CIA MK Ultra mind control methods of using LSD to gather his followers. This story even goes so far as to suggest that the CIA was involved in it.

In this book, our intention is to interview the writers who thoroughly covered the case, as well as those who have written about alternative theories that have captured the interest of true crime enthusiasts. I'm not sure that any of these writers have proven anything different from the standard story that was proven in court. However, this is for you, the reader, to decide after hearing the claims and understanding how they are made.

In the first chapter, we provide a brief review of the crimes and trial for those unfamiliar with the events that preceded the interviews.

PART I
BACKGROUND

The Early Years

Manson was born on November 12, 1934, to his sixteen-year-old mother, Kathleen Maddox, at Cincinnati General Hospital. Even though the last name listed on his birth certificate was "Manson," that wasn't the last name of his biological father. Colonel Walker Henderson Scott Sr. had been with Kathleen Maddox for a short time. After she told him that she was pregnant, Scott stated that he had been ordered away due to his military duties. He left and never returned. It was later discovered that Scott was never really in the army or any branch of the military. Instead, he was a drifter who worked odd jobs at mills or on construction sites. He developed a reputation as a con artist.

Now, alone and only a few months before giving birth to Charlie, Kathleen Maddox began dating and quickly married a man she met at a bar who worked at the local dry-cleaning business, William Eugene Manson. When Charlie was born, they had been married for about three months, so the hospital put his last name on the birth certificate, naturally believing he was the father.

After giving birth, Maddox would spend every day out drinking and partying and leaving the baby with sitters or neighbors. Her husband would eventually leave her and file for divorce in 1937. Only two years after that, Maddox was arrested, charged, and convicted of robbery with assault and sentenced to serve a minimum of five years in prison. Charlie was sent to live with some relatives in West Virginia until Maddox was released on parole in 1942.

After his mother's release, they traveled around to different cities where she continued to drink nightly and get arrested for other crimes. She never had to go to prison again until she met her next husband, Lewis Woodson Cavender Jr., in Indianapolis, Indiana.

With Manson having this kind of youth, it's not surprising that he found himself getting into trouble from as early as the age of nine, when he was caught trying to set his school on fire.

From the age of thirteen, Charlie began being sent to foster homes, schools for delinquent boys, or Catholic Schools for bad kids, where he often ran away. He would end up sleeping on the streets or under bridges. He quickly moved on to committing robbery, as he needed money to buy food or to live. At times, Manson took honest jobs, such as stocking shelves or making deliveries, but he continued to steal to survive.

Manson would first be imprisoned in October 1951, and only one month before his parole hearing, he was caught raping another male inmate and sent to Petersburg, Virginia, to the Federal Reformatory. While there, he continued to commit crimes, including three more sexual assaults on other male prisoners. Finally, he was sent to maximum security in Chillicothe, Ohio, until he reached the age of twenty-one in November 1955.

In the same year, when Manson was released from prison, he met and married Rosalie Jean Wills, who worked at the hospital restaurant as a waitress. Rosalie became pregnant within their first three months together. Manson figured they would do better in Los Angeles, so he decided to steal a car and drive there. Of course, he was caught in Los

Angeles driving the stolen car and arrested. They put Manson on probation for five years. He was then detained for another stolen car charge, but did not appear for his court date. He was sent to prison for three years at Terminal Island in Los Angeles.

During his time in prison, Manson's wife gave birth to their son, Charles Manson Jr. Within one year, Rosalie stopped visiting Charlie in jail because she had met and moved in with another man. By the Fall of 1958, Charlie and Rosalie were divorced. When Manson was released, he married Leona Rae "Candy" Stevens and continued his criminal lifestyle, getting arrested again for theft, but this time, he received a ten-year suspended sentence.

San Francisco

After Manson's release from prison, he first went to Berkley, California. He called the San Francisco probation office, and they assigned him to the supervision of Roger Smith, a federal probation officer working out of the Free Medical Clinic located in the San Francisco Haight-Ashbury district. Manson and the very first people who joined his Family would often go there for treatments, mainly for sexually transmitted diseases.

During the same time, David Smith, the founder of the free clinic, received most of his funding from the National Institutes of Health to study the effects of various drugs on rodents, with the intention of understanding their potential impact on humans. At the time, Smith focused on LSD and methamphetamines, which were popular amongst the counterculture.

During this time, Manson began to take LSD himself, and Roger Smith wrote that he had seen Manson's personality change more abruptly than any other that he had seen during his whole career. The change in Manson brought on his ability to preach to people about a homemade philosophy based on his favorite read at the time, *Stranger in a Strange Land*, which blended elements from the Bible, Beatles songs, and Scientology.

It wasn't long before he began to attract a following of people who were lost and seeking direction. Manson had studied Scientology while in prison, completing 150 hours of auditing. One of his friends, Bruce Davis, was a practicing Scientologist and also worked for the Church.

During his time in San Francisco, Manson met twenty-three-year-old Mary Brunner, a library assistant. Shortly after the meeting, he moved in with her at her tiny apartment. Then Manson ran into a runaway teen named Lynette Fromme, whom he would nickname "Squeaky," and he brought her home to Brunner's apartment and had sex with her.

When Brunner returned home from her job and found the two of them together, she became angry and yelled at Manson, telling him to leave. Somehow, Manson won her back and convinced her not only to let Squeaky stay with them at her apartment but also to allow him to bring home another eighteen different women in the same way he had with Squeaky. She would permit them all to live there with them.

It had become the "Summer of Love" in San Francisco, and numerous spiritual groups were emerging everywhere. Manson was only one of many hippie gurus who preached a particular lifestyle on the streets of Haight-Ashbury. By the end of that summer, Manson had acquired an old school bus and painted it in psychedelic colors, replacing the bench-like seats with large pillows on throw rugs. The group would travel everywhere in this bus around the Los Angeles area, mainly settling down at night on different beaches along the coast.

Mary Brunner gave birth to Manson's son on April 15, 1968, calling him Valentine Michael. Brunner had become a mother-like figure for most of the other girls who were now following Manson. They nicknamed her "Mother Mary."

.   .   .

Rumors Abound

According to author Tom O'Neill, David Smith was also funded by and heavily influenced by the CIA, which was trying to use drugs like LSD to create some mind control. Later, the CIA released their files about what they called "MK Ultra."

O'Neill claimed that Manson learned how to use the drug LSD to control and manipulate his followers into doing whatever he wanted them to do. It was also suggested that the CIA trained Manson in how to do this.

David Smith, in his book *Love Needs Care*, wrote about believing that Manson was attempting to use LSD to reprogram the minds of his followers and use them for different unconventional sexual practices.

Los Angeles

Sometime in the Spring of 1968, Manson moved his Family to the Los Angeles area. In April of that year, while driving, one of the Beach Boys, Dennis Wilson, spotted two hitchhiking young women, Ella Jo Bailey and Patricia Krenwinkel. He picked them up and brought them back to his place. Later that day, Wilson had to attend a recording session, and the girls left. When Wilson returned late that night, he found the girls, Manson, and about a dozen other members of the Family all at his house listening to a Beatles record and doing drugs.

According to Manson's account, this wasn't the first time he had met Wilson. He claimed that he was visiting another friend's house in San Francisco when Wilson invited Manson and his Family to move to Los Angeles and stay at his house on Sunset Boulevard. So, Manson asserted that the reason for them showing up at Wilson's house had nothing to do with Dennis picking up the girls. (Bailey and Krenwinkel)

Over the next few months, Wilson became fascinated with Manson and his music and arranged for him to meet a rock producer friend of his, Terry Melcher. Manson made recordings of his music in Wilson's studio and played a demo for the Beach Boys' record label. The Beach Boys' engineer and producer, Stephen Desper, didn't care for Manson during the session or his music. The Beach Boys would ultimately decide not to record Manson for their label.

After living with Wilson for about six months and after his Family members damaged two of his cars, Wilson decided that he wanted Manson and his Family out. He told them that he was moving out of the house, and they would have to leave as well. Wilson then left to go on tour.

Eventually, Manson moved his Family to Spahn Ranch. Once Manson settled into his new location, he invited producer Terry Melcher to watch him perform an audition. After spending a significant amount of time and money to prepare the place for the audition, Melcher never showed up because, at that time, his stepfather had just passed away, and he had discovered that his mother needed financial assistance. So, he moved out of his rental house and moved into one of his mother's properties. His not turning up angered Manson.

Wilson returned home from his tour, and he had already rented a new place to live out by the beach. He got back into the studio to do some recording with his band and decided he would use one of Manson's songs, "Cease to Exist." During the recording of that song, Wilson ended up changing the arrangement and some of the words. He even gave it a new title, "Never Learn Not to Love."

He had been avoiding Manson now, not only because he was growing tired of him but also because he hadn't told Manson that he had recorded his song. He hadn't given him credit for writing it either. In Wilson's mind, he figured that Manson owed him for not only taking care of him and his Family for six months but also for causing damage to his cars.

When Manson heard about the song, he went looking for Terry Melcher and showed up at his house on Cielo Drive. This encounter is when he met Sharon Tate and her photographer. They told Manson that Melcher no longer lived there.

Next, he went looking for Wilson, and it wasn't long before he located his house. He sent some of his Family members out to do what they called a "Creepy Crawl," where they would break into a home, move things around, and try to freak out the owners. In Wilson's case, Manson also told them to leave a bullet on his front porch.

Lotsapoppa Shooting

When Tex Watson decided that he was going to get some quick cash by ripping off a drug dealer, Bernard "Lotsapoppa" Crowe, Manson got involved. When Lotsapoppa called him at Spahn Ranch and told him that he was coming out there to kill everyone if he didn't get his money back, Manson grabbed another Family member and a gun and went to meet Lotsapoppa at his place.

During an altercation, Manson shot Lotsapoppa in the chest in his apartment. He fled back to Spahn Ranch, thinking that he had killed the man.

The next day, he saw in the newspaper a report that a member of the Black Panthers was shot to death. Manson figured it was the man he had shot, so he figured he had to get everyone ready for when the Panthers came to Spahn Ranch to try and kill them all.

Hinman Murder

Gary Alan Hinman was a thirty-four-year-old music teacher who lived in Topanga Canyon. He was also making mescaline in the basement of his house and would sell it, often to college students and friends. In 1968, Hinman advertised for musicians to join his band. Manson showed up. They hit it off well at first, and he joined Hinman's band. It wasn't long before Manson and some of his girls would stay out at Hinman's house and use his drugs.

One time, when a few of the girls were staying over at Hinman's house, they heard that he was receiving an inheritance of about $20,000. Once they told Charlie this, he came out to Hinman's house to talk him into joining the Family and moving out to Spahn Ranch. Hinman declined the offer.

Manson then sent Bobby Beausoleil, Susan Atkins, and Mary Brunner out to Hinman's to "talk him into" giving them his money. Over three days, they beat and tortured Hinman, trying to get him to give up his inheritance. But he refused, telling them that he didn't have any money.

Beausoleil called Charlie and told them that they were having no luck, so Manson had Bruce Davis drive him out to Hinman's house. Manson sliced Hinman's ear off with a sword. Before leaving, Manson told Beausoleil that he knew what he had to do.

Beausoleil ended up stabbing Hinman to death and, along with Atkins and Brunner, tried to make the murders look like members of the Black Panther Party had committed them. Beausoleil dipped his hand into the bloody stomach of Hinman, placed his bloody palm print on the wall, and then drew three lines above it to look like claw marks. They also wrote words like "Piggie" on the wall in blood.

A week later, Beausoleil was discovered sleeping in one of Hinman's cars, which had been reported stolen after they found the body. Inside the car was also the murder weapon, still covered with Hinman's blood. Bobby Beausoleil was arrested and charged with the murder of Gary Hinman.

Cielo Drive Murders

Manson was panicking about Bobby Beausoleil's arrest. He was worried that Bobby might talk to the police and tell them about Manson shooting Lotsapoppa, whom he still believed he killed. Manson came up with the idea of doing another murder that would look like it was done by the same people who murdered Hinman. A copycat murder.

So, on the night of August 8, 1969, Manson sent Tex Watson out with Linda Kasabian, Susan Atkins, and Patricia Krenwinkel to a house on Cielo Drive, Terry Melcher's old place. It didn't matter that Melcher no longer lived there—the victims just had to be rich and/or famous. The murders needed to make a big splash in the press. Once the police realized that the killers were the same people who killed Hinman, they would let Beausoleil go free.

The group arrived at the house shortly after midnight. It was occupied by twenty-six-year-old Sharon Tate, who was about eight months pregnant, her thirty-five-year-old friend and hairdresser to the stars Jay Sebring, her husband Roman Polanski's childhood friend from Poland, Wojciech Frykowski, and his girlfriend Abigail Folger, daughter of the Folger Coffee Company owner. All four victims had just come home from a late dinner and were all getting ready for bed.

When Watson and his three accomplices arrived at the property, they first spotted Steven Parent, an eighteen-year-old salesman who was visiting the property caretaker that night. He was driving his car out of the driveway and heading home. Watson went over to Steven and, while he was still in his car, shot him four times until he was dead.

Watson broke into the house and entered the living room, where he attacked Frykowski, who was asleep on the couch. Both Krenwinkel and Atkins followed Watson into the house, and he ordered them to locate anyone else who was in the house and bring them out to the living room.

Watson shot Sebring and tied a rope around his neck. After throwing the other end of the rope up over a beam running across the living room ceiling, he tied the other end of the rope around Sharon Tate's neck. He then began to stab Sebring.

Frykowski came to and got loose, running out into the backyard. Atkins chased after him, and when she caught him, she jumped on him and began to stab him. However, Frykowski was too powerful for her. He managed to get away from her, starting to run away. He was yelling for help. When Watson heard the commotion, he ran outside and caught up with Frykowski, jumped on him, shot him twice, and stabbed him to death.

Tate would be the last to die. She asked them to keep her alive until she had her baby and tried to talk them into using her with her unborn baby as a hostage. Neither Watson nor Atkins cared about her pleas, and both began stabbing her until she was dead.

Watson remembered that Manson had told him that they had to leave the murder scene exactly as the Hinman murder scene was left. So, he told Atkins to use Tate's blood and write something on the walls. She ended up writing "Pig" on the front door of the house.

LaBianca Murders

The next afternoon, when Charlie woke up and was looking through the different press reports about the Tate murders, none of them mentioned the Black Panthers in any way. So, he became angry. He devised a plan to find another house among the rich and repeat the same process all over again. This time, though, he was going to go along to ensure things were done correctly.

Manson got into the car, along with Watson, Atkins, Krenwinkel, and Van Houten. They also brought Clem Grogan, a ranch hand at Spahn Ranch, and Linda Kasabian, whom he instructed to drive. They ended up going to the middle-class suburb of Los Feliz, located on Waverly Drive. The house they went to was empty, so Manson chose their neighbor—the LaBiancas.

Manson and Watson entered the house and found Leno LaBianca, who had fallen asleep while reading the newspaper on the sofa. They tied him up and went upstairs and did the same to his wife, Rosemary. While the girls stayed to look after Rosemary, Watson began stabbing Leno to death.

When Rosemary heard what was going on, she began to put up a fight. The two girls couldn't keep her under control. Watson listened to the commotion and ran up into the bedroom and saw Atkins stabbing Rosemary. He tackled her and began stabbing her, too, until she stopped fighting. Watson then ordered Krenwinkel to stab Rosemary as well because Charlie told him to make sure that everyone took part in the murders.

They used the blood of the victims to write "Rise" and "Death to Pigs" on the walls of the living room and "Helter Skelter" (misspelled) on the outside of the refrigerator.

Manson returned to the car and instructed Krenwinkel and Van Houten to go inside and follow Watson's instructions. He then had Kasabian drive them to another house in Venice, which was owned by an actor, Saladin Nader. He told the three of them to get out of the car and go into the man's apartment and kill him. After that, Manson drove back to Spahn Ranch. Kasabian later said that she took the other two to the wrong apartment on purpose as she didn't want to kill Nader. They ended up hitchhiking back home without committing murder.

Shea Murder

Donald "Shorty" Shea was a thirty-nine-year-old Hollywood stuntman who had been working at the Spahn Ranch for the owner, George Spahn, taking care of the horses and property. He was the man who took charge of the ranch and directed all the other employees in their jobs. Manson and Shea didn't like each other from the time they first met.

Manson always believed that Shea was trying to get rid of him. He had heard from several of his Family members that Shea was telling George Spahn to "get rid of all of these hippies," claiming they were bad for business. Any chance that Shea had, he would say something derogatory about Manson in front of everyone.

Around two weeks after the Tate and LaBianca murders, Shea disappeared. Nobody seemed to know where he went. A few times when his name was brought up, Manson said Shea had left for San Francisco because he had gotten a new job there. Manson also claimed that he was the one who told Shea about the job, and this is how he knew for sure that Shea had gone there. Later that year, in December 1977, Shea's remains were discovered off a dirt road in Santa Susana, which was not far from Spahn Ranch.

Ranchhand, Clem Grogan, was arrested that year for murder, and he began talking to the police about things that he was aware of when it came to Manson. Grogan agreed to show detectives where Shea's body was if they gave him a deal on his murder charges.

When Shea's body was discovered, police conducted an autopsy to try to figure out what had happened to him. The medical exam stated that Shea's body had suffered multiple stab wounds, blunt force trauma to the head, and what appeared to be chopping or hacking wounds on the chest.

Later, Manson's accomplice Bruce Davis gave police his account of what happened to Shea.

"We all got into the car on Charlie's orders and went and picked up Shorty. I was riding in the back seat with Grogan, who suddenly pulled out a pipe wrench and began hitting Shorty. Before I knew it, Watson had turned around from the front passenger seat and stabbed him.

Manson pulled the car over, and along with Watson and Grogan, they all dragged Shorty out of the car and down the gravel road far enough where I couldn't see them anymore. I remained seated in the car, saying nothing, for about ten minutes. Then, I decided to get out and follow them down the hill.

When I came up to them, they were all still beating or stabbing Shorty, so I pulled my knife out and did the same. I remember slicing his shoulder, but I noticed he didn't bleed. So, I'm not sure if he was still alive at the time.

Manson then handed me a machete without saying a word. I guess I knew what he wanted me to do with it. All I could do was take the machete and touch Shorty on the back of his neck with it. It wasn't tough enough to cut the skin, so I dropped the machete onto the ground. Manson then handed me a bayonet he brought with him. I took the bayonet and, stabbed Shorty near his right shoulder and yelled, "Are you satisfied, Charlie?"

I dropped the bayonet, then turned around and

walked back to the car, waiting for them to return. I was sick for days after what I had seen and done."

Arrest & Trial & Death

Initially, none of these murders were connected by any of the police detectives working on each case. The Los Angeles Sheriff's Department was in charge of the Gary Hinman murder, and the Los Angeles Police Department was in charge of the Sharon Tate and Cielo Drive murders.

Once the Hinman case detectives heard that similar words had been written in blood in the Tate murders, they contacted the LAPD detectives to tell them that the same thing had been done in the murder they were investigating.

The LAPD detectives ignored the connection between these cases because they were sure that the murders at Cielo Drive happened because of something drug-related, like a bad drug deal or some fake drugs being sold. Then, one of the detectives from the Los Angeles Sheriff's Office, Charlie Guenther, brought up the similarities of these murder cases to prosecutor Bugliosi, who responded to him that the Hinman murder was just a nothing case and he wanted nothing to do with it.

When police first appeared at the Tate residence after their maid had discovered the bodies, they located the property caretaker, Garretson, who had been living in a small gatehouse on the back part of the property. After questioning him at the scene, they arrested him and took him in for further questioning.

Later that same evening, on August 12th, Rosemary LaBianca's son from her first marriage, Frank Struthers, came home from a camping trip that he was on with his friend's family and couldn't get into the house. After getting hold of his sister, who came over with her boyfriend, they were able to get into the LaBianca house and discover the murders.

Along with the press' onslaught of stories concerning the Tate murders, now they had another set of grisly murders to report. They all asked the police about whether these murders were connected. Detectives ruled out any possibility that the same people committed these murders.

Four days later, the police raided the Spahn Ranch in search of stolen vehicles. They ended up arresting Manson and twenty-five of his Family members after discovering several stolen cars on the property. They had been stealing Volkswagen Beetles because they were easy to convert into dune buggies, which they needed to travel in the desert. The police had made a mistake on their search warrant by listing the wrong date, so the charges were dropped, and everyone was released.

In October, after Manson had moved his Family out to Barker Ranch in the desert, the local police and National Park Service there had heard about a gang of hippies living there who were stealing vehicles. As with the first raid, Manson and about twenty-four of his Family members were arrested after they found several stolen cars there. While in jail for the stolen vehicle charges, Susan Atkins began to tell the story about the murders she had been involved in with two of her fellow inmates. Soon after this, her two friends went to the authorities and told them what they had heard. Detectives questioned Atkins, and after she admitted to being involved with the murder of Gary Hinman, she was arrested and charged.

By December 1, 1969, the police announced that they had arrested Tex Watson, Patricia Krenwinkel, and Linda Kasabian for the murders that occurred at

Cielo Drive. They had also arrested Charles Manson and Susan Atkins for the LaBianca murders. Many of them were already in jail from the police raid at the Barker Ranch, and once Kasabian heard she was wanted, she gave herself up.

Police were able to gather lots of physical evidence during their searches, including the gun that Watson used to shoot Steven Parent at the Tate residence. Several of Krenwinkel and Watson's fingerprints were found both inside and outside of the house. There was also a knife that Atkins had used during the murders, which she had lost at the Tate house.

TRIAL

The trial began on June 15, 1970, and was presided over by Judge William Keene. It was one drama after another, with Manson at the center of everything. First, the judge permitted Manson to represent himself at the trial. However, before the trial even began, the judge rescinded that order when, during the pretrial, Manson continued to submit motions that were deemed unacceptable. Manson then filed an affidavit against the judge, claiming he was prejudiced. The judge was replaced with Judge Charles Older.

The testimony phase of the trial began on July 24th, and Manson showed up to court with what looked like an X carved into his forehead. He released a statement saying that the X was there because he had been deemed inadequate and incompetent to defend himself or to speak for himself, as the establishment had "X'd him from the world." The very next day, the rest of his Family members had also marked their foreheads with an X in support of Manson.

The prosecutor, Vincent Bugliosi, ran a case based on the theory that the music of the *White Album* by the Beatles triggered Manson. He claimed that he even left what he thought were messages from the album written on the walls of the victims using their blood. Manson believed that the Blacks were going to rise against the whites in a race war, which he called "Helter Skelter," one of the songs on the album.

When some of the defendants in Manson's Family testified that the reason for both the Tate and LaBianca murders was to create a copycat murder of the Hinman murder, it left the police thinking that Bobby Beausoleil didn't commit that murder, and they set him free. They also testified to this, including writing different words in blood on the victim's walls.

The court atmosphere was like a circus. Several of Manson's followers would show up at the courthouse and cause scenes by lying around on the floor or holding a vigil on the sidewalk outside. They would all have the identical X marked on their foreheads to make people aware of who they were there for. Some of his followers would even carry knives on them in plain view, which was legal to do as long as they were not in the actual courtroom.

Manson's followers also employed a much more aggressive approach with those who were going to testify against Manson. They sent death messages to as many of them as they could find. One of Manson's former Family members, Barbara Hoyt, had agreed to testify for Bugliosi. She was asked to go to Hawaii with Ruth Ann Moorehead, who was still a follower. After arriving, Moorehead got Hoyt a hamburger, which was loaded with hits of LSD. Hoyt was found later on the curb of a road, stoned. Hoyt was taken to the hospital, and when she recovered, she was ready to testify.

A month into the trial, Manson's attorney brought a copy of the *Los Angeles Times* with him into court. The cover story for August 4th was that of President Nixon, who, during his interview for the paper, said that he thought Manson was guilty. Halfway through the day's testimony, the attorney held the newspaper headline up to the jury so that they could all read it.

The judge had to call a hold to the trial so that he could hold a voir dire to see if the jury had been influenced by witnessing the newspaper headline. If they were, he would have to call a mistrial. During the voir dire, it was determined that the newspaper headline did not influence the jury's verdict in the trial.

On November 15th, Bugliosi rested his case and turned the trial over to the defense. After only three days and without calling any witnesses, the defense rested its case. It took another two months for the jury to return with their verdicts. In the early morning of January 25, 1971, the jury convicted Manson of murder, and he was sentenced to death on April 19, 1971.

DEATH

Charles Manson avoided execution. After the California Supreme Court voted in favor of eliminating the death penalty, all death sentences that had been imposed before 1972 would be voided, including the death penalty sentences of the Manson Family. Charles Manson's sentence was commuted to life in prison.

Safely tucked away in prison, Charles Manson lived until the age of eighty-three, when he died from cardiac arrest and respiratory failure caused by colon cancer. He died at 8:13 on the evening of November 19, 2017, at the Mercy Hospital in Bakersfield, California. Manson had been rushed to Mercy Hospital a few times earlier that year due to gastrointestinal bleeding.

PART II
THE INTERVIEWS

Interview with Dianne Lake (Snake)

At the age of fourteen, Dianne Lake was given a note by her parents, who were part of the 1960s hippie revolution. The note granted her permission to be out on her own and not be required to return home. Worthy of note was that her parents never had a home. They sold off everything, and her father converted an old work van into a makeshift camper.

Eventually, she wound up joining the Manson Family, where she stayed for years. We know that her parents were okay with Dianne being part of the Family because one time Manson was arrested, she was with him and, therefore, also arrested. Since she was underage, the police required her parents to come and get Dianne. They wouldn't let

Manson take her since he was neither a parent nor a guardian. Later, after her parents got her released from jail, they met up with Manson, gave Dianne to him, and left.

Dianne ended up spending just over two years with the Manson Family until they were arrested for the murders at the Sharon Tate residence, where she, too, was arrested. After police interrogations, she ended up testifying for the prosecutor during the murder trial.

This interview took place in 2017.

HOM: Let's talk about your early life. You grew up in Minneapolis, correct?

Dianne: Yes.

HOM: It sounds like your parents were into the "Turn on, tune in, and drop out" thing that was going on at the time. How was that for you?

Dianne: Well, it seemed like that's how the world was going. This was the new way of thinking. Bring peace. You know the Vietnam War was not over. There were numerous protests, and people were growing increasingly tired of society and its current state. I believe the counterculture movement was influenced by figures such as Allen Ginsberg, Timothy Leary, and Aldous Huxley, and my dad was particularly drawn to reading their works and listening to their ideas.

Even before we moved to California, he had wanted to visit them there. He wanted to go to Berkley and be part of that. He also wanted to get his Master's degree in art and teach art.

HOM: So, it would seem that during your upbringing, there was a distrust for police and the government, and that was probably how you felt as well. Didn't you want to be part of the mainstream, like schools, police, and government?

Dianne: Right. Now, I loved school, and my education in Minnesota was much better than when we got to California. My parents were disillusioned, which added to the situation. We started taking LSD, smoking marijuana, and listening to Timothy Leary about how LSD was terrific, and everybody should take it.

This led us to get involved with *The Oracle*. This was an underground newspaper in Los Angeles, an offshoot of *The San Francisco*

Oracle, and he wanted to work for them, eventually creating art for them. This led us to join that community. When they (The Oracle Newspaper owners) lost their home, they moved in with us in Santa Monica.

That led some individuals to purchase old bakery bread trucks and convert them into campers. That was supposed to lead us to a communal living experience with the others. This was all in September when I would have been in ninth grade, and I was the oldest of three kids.

HOM: So, all of you were traveling in your camper vans, free as the wind?

Dianne: Yes. We were staying on the beaches. You know, the parking lots of the public beaches on the California coast.

HOM: So, what was it like living that way?

Dianne: It was tight. Five people living in a step-up van. It was a little tight, even though much of your living was outside. I just wanted to help my mom. My mom and dad were arguing—not bad arguments, just topical. They would discuss the roles of men and women in this new era.

But I just wanted to help my mom. One morning, I made pancakes, and she criticized me for not flipping them over. So, I had had it, and so I walked off. I found a little boy who needed a push on a swing. I met his parents, and then I introduced them to my parents. They just drove the bread truck we lived in into their house. Joined forces with them and lived with them for a little while until I thought I heard the voice of God telling me it was time to leave home.

So, I talked to my parents about that, and they wrote me a note. I then moved in with the boy's parents, and my parents moved on. We would meet up again later. Then I met a guy and moved to San Francisco with him because I had a note in my pocket that permitted me. Although it wasn't legal, what fifteen-year-old doesn't feel like an adult?

HOM: Let's talk about when you first met Charles Manson and how you got involved with him.

Dianne: I met him through another couple. My parents had landed in the pot farm commune when I was in San Francisco. I didn't know when I showed up, but they had already made a couple of trips up to Charlie's hog farm. My mom had ultimately given Charlie my photo and said that if you go to San Francisco, look for her. Some of his girls were from the Midwest. My mom thought they were great.

At that point, they were just another commune with a charismatic leader, Charlie. Anyway, this had transpired. I was jailbait. But at that time, the counterculture did not take into consideration what to do with a sexually active underage girl. They were all about sex being good. There was no age. I guess there might have been a time when I was too young, but fourteen was not too young to not have sex.

My parents were just a little bit older. Most parents in the commune were either young or of childbearing age, or they had little kids. There weren't any other kids my age. I didn't have peers in the communes. So, I didn't feel welcome, so I went to live with this other couple, who introduced me to Charlie.

When I walked in the door, Charlie already knew me. I didn't know my mother had given Charlie my picture a month before. So, when I walked through the door, all the girls ran up to Charlie and said, "Look, Dianne's here." I thought, how do they know me? I eventually found out that my mom had given them my picture, but I immediately felt loved and adored.

I didn't join them immediately, but two weeks later, they were getting ready to go on a road trip to New Mexico. I felt loved and adored by them. I loved the girls, and I loved Charlie, and he made me feel extraordinary. And that's how I became a member of the Manson Family.

HOM: When you were still fourteen, you were traveling with Charlie. The police pulled you over, and once they realized you were only fourteen, the police took you in and contacted your parents to come and get you. When your parents arrived, they got you from jail, but then they turned you over to Charlie again. Your parents knew who you were with and must have thought Charlie was okay?

Dianne: Right. Well, he didn't seem any different than all the other commune leaders that were around then. He just became this diabolical person. I don't think murder was on his agenda in that first year. He just turned into it.

HOM: You said that everything was all about love and caring, and you guys would all sit around, take acid, and sing songs. It was all about loving each other. So, when did you first see that it was a change, or when did things begin to change?

Dianne: About a year and a month or two in, and we'd already been going to the desert. Charlie had left me in the desert with another couple to hold down the fort. Unlike other teens, I would help fix the place, gather stones, and decorate the outside.

This was the first time the inner circle had separated me. At least that's how I felt, so when Bobby Beausoleil came by and wanted a girl to help him panhandle, he must have been broke and asked me if I wanted to go with him. So I did. But the whole way, I felt the rocks and the trees crying out at me, and I thought that I had made a mistake. I just felt weird. So when we arrived at the valley, the family was in Gresham Street, a park that no longer existed. There was a whole different vibe going on, and Charlie was distraught with me because I had disobeyed him and not stayed in the desert. So, he said, "You're going back to your parents." That was my punishment, and he found them.

HOM: At that time, did you feel that going back to your parents was a punishment?

Dianne: Yes. It shouldn't have been, but they hadn't kept in touch. I didn't know either that my dad and mom had separated. My mom was not officially married, but was with a different man now. The funny thing is that my dad was still on the scene. It was a mutual thing. They loved each other but couldn't live together—one of those situations.

My mom's new significant other and my dad were the house parents at an alternative boarding school. There were all these girls my age, and my mom had another husband. I was deep into Charlieism and song, and my mind was blown on acid, and I just wanted to climb on the roof and scream out to everybody Charlie's song.

I couldn't relate to these kids my age at all. I wanted to go back, so I found my way back to where Charlie and company were living, and then he took me to Gary Hinman's. Charlie did not want me there with them, and that made me feel horrible.

HOM: How much of this do you attribute to teenage rebellion versus your parents just not being connected or not being able to understand their child, and just releasing them into the wild?

Dianne: The wild back then wasn't as wild as it is now. The media has contributed to that, heightening our awareness of pedophiles, drugs, and all of that. Back in the '60s, we were part of a movement where everybody loved and trusted each other. I was my parents' oldest, and I took some responsibility for what happened. I was the oldest of three. I walked at nine months. I wanted to do everything: iron and wash the dishes. Anything my mom did, I'd do it myself. My nickname was "Do Anne." I was independent, smart, a straight-A student, and loved school. My mom said that I was never happier than when I was going to school. Then you throw in some drugs and some Timothy Leary. My mom and dad were into this new life, and I had asked for emancipation. My parents had given it to me. So, I take some responsibility for that separation. I was on my own. My mom said that I was just like another sister in the commune. I guess they didn't think I needed some direction, supervision, or boundaries.

HOM: How did you get the nickname "Snake?"

Dianne: I had been fasting on lemon honey water, and I just imagined, and I wasn't on acid or anything like that, I just imagined what it would be like to be a snake slithering through the tall cool grass. It was probably a hot day, and I was imagining what it might be like. I relayed that imagination to the girls in the kitchen, and they told Charlie, and that's how I got the name Snake. There's a lot of misinformation out there, but it was just a very innocent tale. An interesting thing is that I was born in the Chinese year of the Snake, too.

HOM: You also got to meet Dennis Wilson and the Beach Boys. Let's talk about that experience.

Dianne: Dennis was an amusing guy. He was cute, and I got to go to the Colorado River with him and two of the other girls in his Rolls-Royce. I just had a bathing suit and a cover-up on it. It was like a family getaway on the Colorado River. Wilson's family wasn't very open to accepting the ragtag girls he brought, but that's who he was. He was the rebel in the family. He liked bringing us ragtag to the family parties. He enjoyed driving fast cars and boats. I loved his house. It was Will Rogers' estate on Sunset. Beautiful grounds, that's what I remember about living there. Big Redwood trees and a big swing were hanging from one of the trees. It was a big log cabin with a pool. It was like living in a park. We used to go to the grocery stores with his Rolls-Royce and go through their garbage dumps to find food, load it up in the trunk, come home, and make him an excellent meal. He used to love that and was very impressed.

HOM: Do you think Wilson had a lot to do with how Charlie changed? There are stories about how Wilson eventually began avoiding Charlie and eventually moved out of his own home to get away from Charlie.

Dianne: His lease was up. He didn't own that house. He moved in with Terry and a few others, and they left. I think his brothers didn't like Charlie either. They did a recording session with Charlie, and I think they tried to mold him into a rock star, but Charlie was not going to be molded. Please do not change the lyrics in his song. Please do not change the way he dresses. In the end, Charlie was disappointed when producer

Terry Melcher came to listen to the demo he had made at the house. Charlie wasn't looking to be a rock star at that point, but he wanted to make some money. Charlie tried to move us all to the desert, so he was looking for money to do that.

HOM: When Charlie Manson first met people, he was often able to enrapture them. What was it about him that captured you when you first met him?

Dianne: Well, he had this uncanny ability to read people. To find out what they needed. It was as if he could see right through you and know your deepest needs and heartfelt desires. Then he could be that or provide that. I don't think he had true empathy. I think he could read people and use it for his benefit.

HOM: What do you think kept you there with him?

Dianne: I think he just made me feel loved and adored. I think they call it "love bombing." It's a manipulation where they shower you with love, affection, and adoration to get you under their power, and then they mistreat you later on. But you still remember the original good feelings. I think that's how Charlie kept me.

That was my biggest weakness facing him in court. Was I going to succumb to those original feelings of being loved and adored by him?

HOM: Were you ever worried about someone trying to get back at you for testifying in court against Charlie?

Dianne: Not really, because I was living with a county sheriff at that point. He took me in as his foster child, so I had protection. I felt safe. When I turned eighteen, I attended junior college and spent two years living in Europe. So, I wasn't worried about that at all.

HOM: You mentioned earlier how close you were to the other girls in the Family. You also said that you weren't aware of the murders that were committed by some of them and Charlie. How did that make you feel later when you found out?

Dianne: I was just shocked that these women, whom I had loved emotionally, and in some cases physically, were capable of this mayhem. It   was   shocking   and   suddenly discombobulated me for the rest of the time that I was in the desert. Hiding from the police the first time the farm was raided was beneficial to me. I was thinking, the whole time that I was hiding under the bush that day, that Charlie would be so proud of me. So, I was still seeking his approval even though he threatened to hang me upside down and skin me alive. I know that he told Tex to kill these people, whoever was in the house. When I think back on it, it was just craziness. That's why I'm so happy to have had the opportunity to write this book and dig deeper.

HOM: You weren't involved in any of these murders, and Charlie kept you distant from them?

Dianne: Yes.

HOM: Do you know why Charlie did this? Was it because of your age or something else? Do you have any ideas why?

Dianne: No. I think it might have been because I wasn't reliable. I was so independent and disobeyed him. I came back from the desert when he told me to stay there, and I didn't. I don't think that I was very trustworthy. Plus, I don't think I could have done that.

HOM: I was going to ask that. How do you think that you would have handled it if Charlie had asked you to participate in the murders?

Dianne: I don't think I could have done it, so would they have killed me because of that? I don't know.

HOM: In the book, you also talk about whenever the Family would get together, Charlie started to play the Beatles' *White Album*. Which was a change from the norm, where everybody sang about love and took drugs. You even wrote that everybody had to pay attention, and it was no longer fun. One time, when you had to go to the bathroom, Charlie wouldn't let you but instead made you go in front of the Family. Even that didn't make you want to leave?

Dianne: Yes, it was embarrassing and humiliating. But I think Charlie had embarrassed and humiliated me enough times before that I was used to it. But it stuck with me because he was setting an example for me. He did not like it if I diverted my attention, like if he had the group's attention all sitting around a circle listening to him talk about whatever was in his mind, what he thought was important to him, and if I would make a flip comment, which I was prone to do, and still do. I know that was part of my personality, but he didn't like that.

HOM: After the arrest, what can you tell us?

Dianne: Well, I didn't tell the police my real name or how old I was for a couple of months. We were all in jail together, and the girls were all together in the same cell. Everyone was admonishing each other not to say anything. It wasn't until Susan Atkins started telling her cellmate in Los Angeles about Charlie and Helter Skelter and her participation in those murders that her cellmate then said to the police. They hauled us all down to Los Angeles County to testify before the grand jury. They were looking for indictments.

After not taking any drugs, eating good food, and reading or overhearing some of the matrons talking about us poor girls and that we were never going to make it, I had all of that as a foundation. When I stood before the bailiff and was about to enter the grand jury, they asked me for my name, age, and other details, which I provided.

I am Dianne Lake, I am sixteen, and I want my mommy. They immediately separated me from the others. That was the first time I had felt safe enough to tell them my real name and age. Up until then, I had been arrested in Ventura County with a fake ID, and I was using that. But they were much nicer and kinder to me once they knew my real name and age. Before that, they were much rougher and constantly threatened with the gas chamber and other things. So, they softened me up and sent me to a mental hospital, and it was a good experience. They were able to deprogram.

HOM: How do you think it would go today if you saw Charles Manson?

Dianne: I can't just go visit him. I have to submit paperwork, and he must approve my visit. But if I had the opportunity to visit him and had one question, I would ask him, "Did he believe that he was Jesus Christ?" I think that was pivotal for him and us, that we believed he was some messiah. He would often reiterate that his name, Manson, was no accident. That he was God's son. I think that's why he got the *White Album* by the Beatles. He believed they were sending him a message because he was the second coming.

HOM: How do you feel about him now, honestly?

Dianne: He's crazy. I could say he's a psychopath, you know. He loves that. But he's just crazy. I am sure that he loves being the icon of evil. It's exciting to him.

HOM: How do people receive you now?

Dianne: I'm worried about what I call the whackdoodles. I'm concerned about the people who are obsessed with this case and think they know everything there is to know about it. Those are the only negative reviews I get.

Listen to the full interview with Dianne Lake on my website:

https://www.alanrwarren.com/house-of-mystery-episodes/episode/b44d25e5/dianne-lake-snake-member-of-the-manson-Family

Interview with Marlin Marynick

Charles Manson was looking to make a movie, and when he heard that a psychiatric nurse had connections to the film industry, he decided to reach out to him. Marlin Marynick was a nurse who had been working in prisons for over twenty years in Regina, Canada. Marlin considered their meeting to be more surreal than scary, as he had grown up hearing the many stories in the press about the Manson Family and their notorious murders. He figured that Manson was probably one of the main reasons he got into a psychiatric career.

Marynick ended up writing a book, *Charles Manson Now*, which covered the years that the two men were in contact. Most of their conversations happened over the phone, with Manson calling from prison. Over the years, there were only a few times when the two men were unable to talk. Those were the times when Manson had done something that caused the prison to take away his privileges, such as using a phone to call somebody. The last time Marynick spoke with Manson was about eight months before his death.

We were able to interview Marlin Marynick in February 2018, just three months after Manson's death. In the interview, we were able to cover several of their conversations, most of which he has on tape.

HOM: Who is Marlin Marynick?

Marlin: I work in psychiatry; I'm part of a crisis response team that works in my city, and I've been doing that for over twenty years.

HOM: So, Manson called you out of the blue?

Marlin: Yes. We had a mutual friend. His name is Donald Taylor. We were working on a film project with him. At the time, Taylor was trying to publish a book which was about a gay man who had all of these exploits with some popular people, like James Dean, the Duke of Windsor, and even Charles Manson was one of the people in his book. Charlie had kept in touch with him since before the murders.

I was on eBay, and someone was selling some of James Dean's hair, a shirt that belonged to Elvis, and some letters written by Charles Manson. I contacted the seller of these items, and we ended up becoming friends. He was also acquainted with Charles Manson, and it was through working with him that Manson became aware of my work in Canada on a film project.

He wanted to do this interview to make some money, so he called me. When he called, he asked if I would dress up like a soldier and he would dress like a General, and we would do this interview. I told him that I could do that. But the California prison system wouldn't allow it to happen. So, we tried elsewhere. The BBC was close to taking action, but it never happened. We kept in touch and became friends, and I eventually met with him. All of that eventually turned into a book.

HOM: When you first got this call from someone who said they were Charles Manson, did you believe it right away?

Marlin: It was weird, and I had a roommate at the time. But when you hear his voice, it's pretty unmistakable. He has a kind of language that only he can speak. It was a weird interview. He wanted to know about life in Canada—where I lived, and what I did. He also asked my thoughts on insects. I remember that because I thought it was pretty weird. I told him that I liked spiders and crickets. About an hour after the call, I received a call from his assistant, Gray Wolf, and we began trying to figure out how to conduct the interview.

HOM: That's how it started. And for people who don't know, you recorded your conversations with Manson?

Marlin: Yes. I missed recording some of the early conversations with him because I wasn't thinking to record them. He suggested that I do that because of his history. That's his words. Eventually, I started to record them.

When I met with him, which was about a year after we first spoke on the phone, he hadn't seen anyone for about two or three years because he doesn't socialize with people. The first time I went to meet him, the prison wouldn't allow me in. They thought I had forged documents, as they couldn't believe he had a visitor. I had to return four months later after I got approval from the warden.

When I finally got in to meet him, he was still focused on making a film of an interview with him. I asked him about writing a book about him. He said that was bullshit because there were already about four hundred books written about him. The idea was that he wanted to write an exclusive book, and he wanted me to be his biographer. He needed six hours to complete everything he needed to do to get it to me.

I don't know if you recall the media coverage when he was caught with cell phones. He did that because prison calls are recorded, and he didn't think that he could say what he wanted to say. So, in the end, he said that I just had to write about myself and use those recorded phone calls. So, that's what I used in the book, and that's his dialogue.

So, we can't figure each other out. He can't understand how someone can hold a job and be responsible, and I can't figure out how he can live in a prison. A significant portion of my experience with him involved him educating me about the prison system, his upbringing, and his life experiences, including his childhood and similar aspects.

I was over my head when it came to the murders and that whole rabbit hole, so I just tried to work with him as a person and tried to figure out why this guy was so relevant, why he was so influential.

HOM: What was the first thing that you asked Manson?

Marlin: I know everyone thinks he's some master manipulator and that kind of thing. From my end, I thought, "Holy shit, this is my boogeyman." When I was a kid, I found a beat-up copy of *Helter Skelter*. I used to play in a band in houses, and I remember seeing it in a basement that scared the hell out of me when I was eight or nine. I couldn't understand the content, but I remember those eyes. When you get into psychiatry, you follow him. At his parole hearing, I began watching the interviews and clips of his music, and I started learning about the man.

But I never thought in a million years that I would get to sit down with the guy and talk about The Doors and whatever. I think if you planned that with him, it would go south, and it just wouldn't happen.

HOM: Was there anything that surprised you about him during the interview when you were speaking with him, or was there something that caught you off guard?

Marlin: Well, you know the people who do intense jobs? Like surgeons or police or EMTs, there's a kind of gallows humor. Prison humor is a lot more graphic. He is the most direct person that I have ever met. And the most complex. For instance, if he has a problem with you, he lets you know about it.

Time is different for him. I think the one thing I found most fascinating was that he would tell you that he spent eighty percent of his life in prison. But he counts foster care, boys' homes, and all of those kinds of things as being in prison as well. Sixty percent of that time was in solitary confinement. Most of that is self-imposed because he can't deal with people.

So, this idea of the way he lives in his head so much, and he has this inner world, and I know he has some mental health problems or other concerns, you could say. I want to be careful about how I word that, but he's been through a lot of trauma and seen a lot of stuff. Living in that environment and that violence and how he made it through all of that, it's pretty amazing, the guy's a total survivor.

HOM: Did he ever talk about his Family?

Marlin: Yes, and like with everyone else in his life, he has a love-hate thing. I got a letter from him once, and he wrote that I was the stupidest person that he had ever met, and how could I even stay alive being as retarded as I am. It was scathing and somewhat weird. This guy receives thousands of letters a week, and he takes the time to tell me how stupid I am. However, when he called, I said to him that I had received his letter, and as it turned out, he apologized for it. The way he apologizes is a little different. People play him, and people try to get favors. There's a whole industry surrounding him.

He always tried to explain the prison world, and I tried to explain to him what it was like living out here. To him, the way we live is speedy. He can't relate to the pace. Every time he got out of jail, it had doubled or tripled, and it was too crazy. He never really wanted to get out.

I asked him what he'd do, and he said that he'd sit down and look around for a while, which I thought was a pretty good answer. Significant changes have occurred, including advancements in technology. One thing that happened when we were working on this interview was that he got a flat-screen TV, which became prison-issue. He tried to send me his old TV, and I don't know what happened. I never got it.

But he saw on TV someone using Skype, which allows you to talk on your TV to someone else, enabling you to communicate back and forth. He would go on rants about this. Once, when I was visiting and a guard walked by, Charlie said, "You see that guy?" and I replied, "Yeah." He said, "Well, that asshole is mocking me all the time." I asked Charlie what he was mocking him about, and he said the guy was always holding his cell phone up towards Charlie because he didn't have one. I told Charlie that he was probably taking pictures of himself. That didn't occur to him.

HOM: Well, the world changed so much from when he was put in prison.

Marlin: Oh yeah. Charlie sent me a bunch of his fan mail, and I read the content of what he got. Everybody wants something from him, such as students writing papers or those who sent him ten dollars and asked him to sign a receipt or some paper, trying to get an autograph. The way he would screen people was quite impressive. When you think of a celebrity, he isn't, and he doesn't carry himself that way at all.

HOM: So, he didn't talk to you about any of the crimes?

Marlin: We had an excellent fight once. I had given an interview somewhere where I said that if I knew what was going to happen, and in my world, if you knew that there was going to be violence on that kind of level and you did nothing to prevent it, you would have to be accountable in some way. Charlie was adamant that that was not the case. However, it doesn't work that way. Philosophically, I struggle to relate to that. Morals and righteousness are significant concepts.

When the book came out, Charlie was in the hole at the same time, and the person who was in the cell next to him read the whole book to him. Charlie's response was surprising because I didn't exploit certain things, and he just assumed that's what I would do, as that kind of thing happens to him all the time.

HOM: Well, if he's had that kind of thing happen to him all the time, you can understand why he thought that way.

Marlin: Yes, and he's dealt with lots of even top-tier people like *Dr. Phil*, *Inside Edition*, and shows like that. Those people are all vultures. It's unbelievable; there's not a whole lot of ethics.

We talked earlier, just before we went on air, about the whole funeral (Manson's) thing. And all the arrangements around it. I know all of those parties, everyone involved, and who's fighting to do what's right with the remains of Charlie, and it's a circus. I can see why the public is interested, but it's somewhat disheartening that it's come to this.

HOM: Did he ever talk to you about his kid, grandkid, and pen-pals? Who did he like or didn't like?

Marlin: Yeah, Matthew Roberts, who I still consider to be a good friend. Every time I've been to California, he's taken me out, and we do stuff together. He's not Charlie's son, and he knows that. So, I don't understand why they're moving forward with this fake documentation, claiming it's Charlie's will. His grandson, I've spoken to on the phone. He means well. I wish that he and Channels would get together and do that media-free. I'm sure they could work out their differences and come to a compromise. The will that Michael Channels has is Charlie's writing and direction, and it's 100 percent authentic as far as I can tell.

HOM: What are the most significant differences between these guys?

Marlin: I think the thing about the whole Manson mystique is that he's becoming an outlaw and kind of a poet, or sage, even a shaman to a lot of people. Many artists and people are clinging to the different parts and the whole "innocence" thing and advocating for Charlie's freedom. It's this entire imagery thing. He doesn't get paid anything. Everyone takes advantage of him all the time. Even when he was alive, they used his image and his voice to sell everything. So, I think it's owning that copyright and controlling his music is another thing. He thought the primary interest that I had in him was his music. He knew that Mama Cass wanted to testify on his behalf at his trial, and Neil Young gave him a motorcycle. He was friends with everybody.

When he was in prison, he thought people like Bing Crosby were rock stars. That's who he aspired to be. Creepy Carpus taught Manson how to play guitar in prison. Creepy was a member of the Barker Gang, led by Ma Barker. So, he had the basics down and understood how to structure a song and how to play. That's what he was going to do. All the prison staff encouraged him and believed he possessed this ability. When he got out of prison, he went to Whiskey and saw the Grateful Dead play, and then he decided to throw his guitar away, as he couldn't believe what it had evolved into.

HOM: Why do you think things about Manson sell so well?

Marlin: I think he hits on every level. You have the true crime thing and the mystery behind that, the mind control and the cult thing, the hippie cult leader thing. You also have the music, and then there's the art he creates and that kind of thing.

When I visited him, he was constantly tapping on the table, as if he were fidgety all the time, and kept his back against the wall. He was pretty paranoid. He had an obvious sense of rhythm, and you don't just have that. It's a developed thing. I asked him if he ever played drums, and he said yes, for four years in San Quentin. He would lower and raise the water levels in his toilet to achieve different pitches, and he would use those as drums. Somehow, he acquired an old toilet seat and found some string or wire, and he was able to tune a weird harp-like guitar. So, all of that kind of stuff, and I think if you are a loner or outcast, they are naturally drawn to that because he's almost a poster child for that.

HOM: Did Manson express his hate for anyone?

Marlin: He hated parts of what I do, especially psychiatry. For four or five years, they used heavy antipsychotics as a chemical restraint to calm him down. He was so medicated that he couldn't do much. He just drooled. The side effects of those medications are very harsh. He always feared getting put into a psych ward or something like that because of those memories of being drugged.

When you asked him what he had, he would say everything. ADD, FAS, Head injury, schizophrenic, bipolar, you know everything. The one thing that he wouldn't admit to, which is still fascinating to me, is depression. He never understood suicide or how anyone could do that. He said that the most disturbing mail that he gets is all of those from people saying, "Charlie, you're the only reason I'm alive," or "If it weren't for you, I would have killed myself." He doesn't get it at all. He doesn't understand fandom. He couldn't understand why people thought he was in a good position or would want his autograph.

Charlie went through the prison system and ended up in Baskerville, where there was a Harry Krishna guy who was chanting. Charlie and the guy got into a fight where the guy ended up throwing paint cleaner on him and then lighting him on fire, and he almost died.

That's when they decided that Manson was a high-profile inmate and he was going to get killed because some other inmate was trying to make a name for themselves. So they made this unit called PHU. This is where he was housed when I met him. It's like a celebrity inmate unit, and it's very low-key. There are always fewer than twenty people housed in there at a time. I believe there were only fourteen during my visit. People like Sir Han. There were other serial killers and deviant sex offenders that people would write books about. The man who killed Bill Cosby's son was in that unit, too. So, it was a little different environment because they also had free rein. They could have things like a guitar, but they were protected, which he liked. He lived by the old school prison code. You know that was everything to him, and he would tell you that he was going with all the secrets.

HOM: What kinds of secrets do you think that he had?

Marlin: I asked him directly, "Did you know what was going to happen?" He tells me that he wasn't there very often and that he wasn't a leader. He was a follower. He got out of prison, and he was in Hate Ashbury, in the middle of the hippie movement. And he knew how to read people and how to work people. Absolutely, he's a pimp. He's done all of that shit. He knows how to survive in prison. He's not stupid. He knows how to do all of that. So, he was looking for an underpass or somewhere to sleep, and these kids said to him, "Stay with us." He thought this was utterly insane. Three years ago, these kids would have been terrified by him, and that would have never happened. But now there was a movement. So, he fell into it. The timing was perfect for that to happen.

I think that he felt some level of responsibility. When I started talking to him, and things were getting out of hand, a pending race war was underway, and he said he didn't like the Beatles, which is disputable. The *White Album* was telling him that he needed to dig this hole underground. To me, that's a guy who has a nervous breakdown or a psychotic break. I don't see any mastermind behind any of that.

The hippie movement was only about six or eight months, and then it all started to become exploitative and opportunistic. People were all flocking from all over America and Canada, and they were all trying to find this idealized lifestyle, which is very easy to be victimized in. There are all kinds of murders, overdoses, and rapes. It was just crazy.

HOM: Yes, I heard that the Manson Family was only one of many families like that going on back then.

Marlin: Yes, there were several. With that lifestyle, you essentially have groupies, hangers-on, and similar individuals, which is a relatively new phenomenon. It was the late 1960s in California. Charlie knew how to work and exploit that. He knew those guys would go where girls are, and girls are power. He used that to end up with Wilson (Beach Boys), and he started to try to record a record.

HOM: What did Manson tell you about that time and the Beach Boys?

Marlin: What Charlie told me about all of that was that he recorded and brought in everybody, and he thought that they could capture something live and memorable. He didn't understand the concept of taking and redoing things at all. Any engineer is likely to be frustrated working with him. You can't work with him. So, that fell apart.

The girls were all partying with the celebrities and actors, and Hollywood was convoluted with all of these people. And all of these drugs were flowing around, and then all of the stupidity. Then you had a guy named Polanski, who got a device called a VCR, which was state-of-the-art and had never existed before. You could make home movies, and they could watch them. I've heard about some of the films that exist and are out there, so I talked to Charlie about that. He knew all of it and said Sharon Tate was his friend, and he would often go swimming in her pool. So, these guys all knew each other, and that's not at all what I thought. The Tate house was a well-known drug house.

Tex Watson was a drug dealer, a very bad one. He shot people and ripped people off, and nobody wanted to do anything about it. Whatever you are doing, you are somewhat aware of what your colleagues or competitors are doing as well. They all knew that the Tate house was expecting a shipment of items, and Jay Sebring, a hair stylist known as the

Candyman, would go around cutting people's hair and drop off drugs to them.

I'm told that Tex Watson went over to the Tate house trying to schmooze them because he wanted to be part of the drug shipment. They didn't know what to do, so they said, 'Tex, come back in an hour or so."

Tex went and found Charlie and told him that this should be their drug deal, and Charlie responded to him by saying, "Do what you're going to do and shut the fuck up." That's what he said happened. It was a home invasion. I do not doubt that they all knew each other, and it wasn't about a bad record deal or anything like that. But I think it's all tied together, and it's a lot of drugs and a lot of personalities.

HOM: How well did Charlie know Roman Polanski?

Marlin: That I don't know. I never asked him. That would have been a good question, but he said he knew Sharon (Tate). I have heard reports that she had been out at the Spahn Ranch riding horses when Charlie was there.

HOM: Was there ever a time when Charlie scared you?

Marlin: Well, he was pushing eighty when I met him, so not really.

HOM: It's just that quite often in interviews and with the media, he would act tough, really mean, and say things like, "If I wanted you dead, you'd be dead. I could have you killed anytime."

Marlin: Yeah. He would say things like, "I can have someone knock on your door in three days." So, is that a threat, or is that how cool I am? Or he said, "Are you Scared?" and I'd say, "No," and he'd say, "Well, you should be."

People would ask me how they should write to Charlie so that he would respond. You would get a better response telling him about your cat than asking him about the murders, you know? That's kind of how he was.

He told me that Marilyn Manson had been trying to get in touch with him for the longest time, but he always wrote from a P.O. Box instead of an actual personal address. So, he said, who the fuck does this guy think that he is? Manson feels that you are hiding something from him when you do that. You need to include your address so that he knows where you live, that kind of thing.

I've had some pretty good rants from him. There was one time when I was supposed to visit him, but I was in California at the time. He called the night before. Sometimes, he would get paranoid, or there might be issues with other inmates, or he just didn't want to leave his cell. That happens. It was just one of those times when I was there, and he didn't feel that he could come out to see me. After I got home, I told him that it would have been good to see you when I was there. He then went off on me and said, "You're lucky I didn't see you. I would have jumped on your back and slit your throat. He was way overreacting.

HOM: Did he ever talk about the girls who were in his Family?

Marlin: Yes, he did. I think it's because it was on his mind a lot, but I believe, in many ways, his life stops when the prison door closes. His reference points are all from the sixties.

HOM: Did he ever say that he felt betrayed

by some of the girls in the Family, as a few of them testified against him?

Marlin: Well, it depends. Even his mother, depending on the day, can sometimes be a saint and, at other times, the worst person on the planet. He was careful when he spoke with people to ensure that there was nothing possessive about it. When we were writing the book, he would say, "You should put this in the book," and I would say, "Okay, I'll do that." Then he would say, "I'm not telling you to do it." He was trying to avoid the whole command thing.

The girls would come up a little bit, but I didn't know enough about them. None of them were supposed to communicate because they committed a crime, but I'm not sure that happened. There were outside people who would rewrite their letters and send them. So, he was on top of what everyone was doing.

One of the more unusual aspects was his reverence for the uniform and his respect for authority and the military. I always thought that he was a big hippie or a punk who was out of society, but I didn't see it that way at all. If you ever spoke badly about a soldier, he would take that personally. He felt very strongly about it.

HOM: What do you think was the most important thing that you learned from your time interviewing him?

Marlin: As time goes by, I have way more respect for the guy. He tends to do his own thing. He's all about righteousness and respect and honor and those kinds of values. And that's kind of what he took to his grave.

We were talking about when the murders happened, and he said I can't believe they killed her. She was a beautiful woman, and what a waste of life. He could have played it that way, but he told me that he didn't think this was going to happen because he knew he wasn't there. Everyone knows he wasn't there, and that's easy to prove.

He didn't think that he was going to end up on death row. And if he had known, you would have seen a much different Charles Manson. He was showboating, and he was getting attention.

HOM: Let's say that, indeed, he didn't know anything about them going to murder the Sharon Tate household, or how it was going to go down. How about the other murders that also happened on different dates, such as the LaBianca murders?

Marlin: It goes beyond that to the Bobby Beausoleil murder. I'm not sure exactly what happened there, but he was the most attractive male in the group and the one all the girls fawned over. There's a theory that, in trying to get him out of jail, they wanted to stage the Sharon Tate murder. I think there's an element of truth to that. I think it was a drug deal, but the writing with blood on the walls was like a copycat murder. Additionally, the daughter of LaBianca was directly involved with the Family.

One thing that Charlie told me was that Angela Lansbury signed her daughter over to him when she was only fourteen or fifteen. Although that sounds completely unbelievable, if you conduct a little research, you'll find out that it happened. One of the weird stories he told me was when they went to Angela's house and robbed her, because that's what they did, they stole all of her fur coats. And he had a dune buggy where he glued some of these furs onto it. He also found some horns and placed them on the front of the buggy. When he was telling me this story, he was laughing his ass off.

However, it was a different time. The police worked differently, and it was a completely different world. Even though they were robbing A-list celebrities, they were still eating out of garbage cans. But at the ranch, they would all bring him art and paintings, and they all disappeared after the ranch was raided. Charlie wanted to know what happened to all of that stuff.

Listen to the full interview with Marlin Marynick on my website:

https://www.alanrwarren.com/
house-of-mystery-episodes/
episode/b4772a05/manson-
tapes-marlin-marynick

Interview with Ivor Davis

Ivor Davis is an American-based foreign correspondent who believes the Beatles didn't make them do it. The interview took place on April 19th, 2022.

HOM: What got you into this story?

Davis: I was, at the time, the West Coast correspondent for one of the most prominent London newspapers, called the *London Daily Express*. In that role, I was tasked with covering a wide range of both major and minor stories. I was covering the 1969 moon landing. I was covering the speech of Bobby

Kennedy in the kitchen where he was shot, so I am handling some of the biggest stories.

Then, in August 1969, the office called me from London and said there was a story on the wires. The wire services were putting out a story saying there were some murders in a very respectable area of Beverly Hills, in Cielo Drive, and to get over there and tell them what's going on, who the victims were, and as much as I could, because they know very little about them.

So, off I went. I lived about twenty minutes away from Beverly Hills' Cielo Drive, in the canyon of a very respectable neighborhood. When I arrived, the media were gathered outside the house's gates, and we didn't know what was going on. As the day wore on, the horrific details of what had happened there began to emerge.

We discovered the murder of the eight-month-pregnant actress Sharon Tate and her friends, including Jay Sebring, who was a celebrity hairstylist to some of the biggest names in Hollywood. They were all dead, and we didn't know how. We just hung around and hung on every little piece of information. Plus, the fact that, as you can imagine, with communications not the way they are today, with no internet, rumors were wild. We wondered who had been murdered and why they had been murdered. And the stories that came out were pretty wild for the first few days.

HOM: What were some of the first stories like? When you heard that Sharon Tate was murdered, what did people believe at first?

Davis: First of all, I was pretty shocked as I knew Sharon, and I interviewed her on the *Valley of the Dolls* movie, which had come out about a year earlier. She was an up-and-coming star at the Twentieth Century Fox Studios. The stories were wild. First of all, they said it was a mob hit, second, they said it was some orgy involving drugs, and another was a drug deal that went wrong. So much wild stuff and so many stories, maybe the Ku Klux Klan, because some of the bodies supposedly had white hoods on them.

So, you can imagine it was a festering mass of rumors, and none of us could sort it out until we eventually obtained the names of the people. Even then, it took a considerable amount of time for the truth to come out.

HOM: What, if any, do you think the relationship was between Sharon Tate and Charles Manson? Did they know each other, and was this a planned murder?

Davis: In my opinion, he didn't know who she was. He may have spotted her at the house once when Terry Melcher, the son of Doris Day and a record producer, became a friend of Manson's and promised to give him a recording contract. He had lived in the house before Sharon Tate did. In my opinion, Manson didn't know who lived in the house.

Manson had sent Tex Watson and some of the girls to kill everyone who was in the house. It's a somewhat complex story, but in my opinion, the reason Manson did the murders—he ordered the murders of Sharon Tate, and twenty-four hours later, the murders of Leno and Rosemary La Bianca—was because he was trying to cover up the murder that happened on July 27th, two weeks before the Sharon Tate murder of a guy called Gary Hinman, a musician who Bobby Beausoleil murdered. Bobby Beausoleil was a friend of Manson, who was also a musician who had killed Gary Hinman at the instructions of Charles Manson.

Mr. Beausoleil was sitting in prison, facing first-degree murder charges and the gas chamber. Manson felt that he was the one who sent him out to kill Hinman, so, believe it or not, and a lot of people dispute this, but with my experience and my investigation, Manson set up these two senseless killings to try to take the heat off Bobby Beausoleil. The cops would look at the murders of Sharon Tate and the murders of the LaBianca and say, "Hey, I don't think we've got the right guy for the murder of Gary Hinman because there's a gang of black militant killers out there who are murdering people, so Mr. Beausoleil should be set free." I mean, it's a crazy, crazy theory. But that's the one I believe to be the truth.

However, as you know, and the world knows, Vincent Bugliosi, the prosecutor, came up with a new theory. He claimed that Manson brainwashed his disciples to believe that the Beatles' *White Album* songs like "Helter Skelter," "Piggies," and "Revolution" were the real reason. There's a secret message to tell Charlie to kill so that they can start a race war, and Charlie would escape, having been forewarned that there was going to be a race war. I mean, as we talk, Alan, and as you're listening, I'm sure some of your listeners are saying this guy is crazy, and this theory is mad. But I honestly believe that was the true theory for the murders. That it was a cover-up, it was to throw cops off the scent of Manson's close ally Bobby Beausoleil.

HOM: We had one of the Manson Family members on the show, Dianne Lake, or she was called "Snake" by Manson. She said that Charlie would play the *White Album* every day over and over. So, was he doing that for some reason, even though he had something different planned in his mind?

Davis: I mean, Dianne Lake wrote a terrific book. She was a young woman, as you know. She was fourteen when she was turned over to the clutches of Manson. She and everybody that I spoke to soon after the murders and the arrests were made also said to me that "Charlie brainwashed us. Charlie played the *White Album* over and over, and he made us believe in it." I think he made them feel that Dianne took heavy drugs or was given heavy drugs, but I know many members of the Manson Family were under the influence of LSD, mescaline, and other medicines that Manson handed out.

So, I have no doubt whatsoever that, as Dianne Lake probably told you, the members of the Manson Family believed the theory that the Beatles were telling Manson and giving him a method for this race war. They thought it was because they had been brainwashed to accept it. So, I don't dispute that argument, but I can tell you that I traveled with the Beatles in 1964 and got to know them very well on their first American tour. I knew the lyrics of the Beatles' music, and I thought, how could a song like "Helter Skelter" be perceived as a blueprint for a race war? I mean, come on, look at the lyrics, listen to the lyrics, and some of the other songs could be so twisted out of fashion, but they believed it because Manson was an incredible snake oil salesman.

HOM: The song "Helter Skelter" was about a ride at a fair, correct?

Davis: It was. In England, there was an up-and-down ride on a fairground that Paul McCartney wrote the song about. But the other thing that adds up to this kind of outrageous motive for the murders is that Manson looked at the Bible and said there were the four horsemen of the apocalypse.

They were wearing breastplates, and they had the hair of women. He said to his demented followers, "Well, the Beatles have the hair of women. The Beatles have breastplates, except they don't call them breastplates, they call them guitars." Manson reinforced this thesis. As I said, they began to believe it.

Soon after the arrest, I spoke to Paul Watkins and Brook Poston, and they believed this crazy Beatles theory. The remarkable aspect is that Vincent Bugliosi used that as the foundation of his prosecution, and he persuaded a jury to accept it. They convicted Manson because if they hadn't convicted Manson, who knows?

Suppose they had gone with the theory that I mentioned, which was two murders, to throw the police off the scent for the murder of Gary Hinman. In that case, Manson might have gotten off free, and Bugliosi didn't want to risk that, so he went with the most outrageous motive, and he got away with it. He got convictions.

HOM: So, do you think that Bugliosi thought the same theory that you do, but just went with the Helter-Skelter theory because he knew that would get Manson convicted?

Davis: I think that's right. Here's what happened, and it may sound self-serving, but in 1970, before the trial began, I had written a very brief book outlining the blueprint of the *White Album* and the lyrics of the song. Years later, Aaron Stovitz, who had once been the lead prosecutor before falling out of favor and Bugliosi stepping into the number one chair, told me that Bugliosi had obtained your book and used the "Beatles made me do it" theory. When he said that to me, I thought maybe this was sour grapes because Stovitz was once the lead prosecutor, and Bugliosi replaced him.

So, I always thought it was a somewhat dubious motive. But the fact is, it worked. It got the prosecution to make the jury believe that that was the reason for the murders. Whatever you say today, in retrospect, you've got to give Bugliosi credit, as he got the convictions even though we all thought that it was a pretty crazy motive.

HOM: Let's talk about the relationship between Manson and Terry Melcher and the Beach Boys. What was it really like, and how did that go down?

Davis: This was the interesting thing. When Manson was in prison, he learned to play the guitar. Upon his release, he started writing music and made a concerted effort to connect with other people in the music industry, as he aspired to become a rock star. As it turned out, Manson instead became the most notorious killer since Jack the Ripper.

Along the way, Manson became connected to Dennis Wilson of the Beach Boys, who lived in a brilliant mansion on Sunset Boulevard. Poor Dennis was one of the neglected children of the Beach Boys. He wanted more acknowledgment from his brothers.

Dennis ran into Manson, and they spoke the same language. They were both into music, and Manson had conned Mr. Wilson so much that Manson and his Family moved into Dennis' house for several months. Wilson got all the sex and drugs that he wanted, which were provided to him by Manson. Dennis repaid Manson by bringing all the rock stars to his mansion, where they would be forced to listen to Charles Manson singing and auditioning every night. Manson auditioned for John Phillips of the Mamas and the Papas, Cass Elliot, and Neil Young, among others.

They all flocked to Dennis Wilson's house, and Manson was thrilled, as he now had an international audience of rock stars.

It was also because he was a friend and houseguest of Dennis Wilson that Manson met Terry Melcher, who was at the time seeking new talent, and that's how they came together. Manson knew that Melcher lived on Cielo Drive, and he also later learned when Melcher moved out of the house on Cielo Drive. So, the idea that Manson would send killers to the house on Cielo Drive to get revenge on Melcher because Terry never gave him a recording contract is not valid, in my opinion.

Another thing was that, due to his closeness to Dennis Wilson, Charles Manson had written a song called "Ceased to Exist" and gave it to Wilson to use on a Beach Boys album. Wilson put it on the album and also made a single out of it. But Wilson changed the name of the song and never gave Manson credit for it. Manson was royally angry over that.

HOM: Was Manson kicked out of Wilson's house?

Davis: Yes, he was. Here's what happened. Poor Dennis Wilson was out of control. He was into drugs, he was into booze, he was into sex, and he became beholden to Manson because Manson provided him hot and cold running sex with the girls. When Manson told his girls, "You sleep with this person or that person," the girls obeyed. It was akin to candy to a child. That was Dennis Wilson.

Dennis Wilson finally threw up his hands, went to Brothers Records, and said to the guy who was running the show, "Look, I'm leaving my house, and I want you to get rid of these people that I can't get rid of. Dennis Wilson then left him out at a friend's house in Malibu, while the brothers' record executives ended up evicting Manson and the girls from the house. That was the only way they could get them out of the house. Wilson then became somewhat fearful of Manson. Dennis Wilson believed that when Manson was arrested, Manson was out for revenge for him as well. So, a lot of paranoid behavior from everyone.

HOM: Being as you were around the scene from the beginning, are there some things that the public might not be aware of when it comes to Charles Manson?

Davis: This story is complex and has so many leading characters. One of the saddest characters in this was Roman Polanski. Polanski, as some people are aware, is still active, and he has just completed a new film in France, which could be a contender for the Best Foreign Language Film Oscar next year. Polanski has won an Oscar already, but that was after the murders.

So, Roman Polanski is married to this gorgeous actress, who's expecting his first child. And then he's called while in London, telling him that she's dead, along with his unborn baby. He came to L.A., and I was there when he arrived. He is distraught, absolutely beyond himself, as one would expect. He thinks at the beginning that somebody in the show business circle, maybe even his friends, was responsible for the murder of Sharon. The cops are clueless at the time, and they haven't solved the case for four months. So, Roman Polanski, who'd gone through the horrible World War II, lost his mother in a concentration camp. His father was also in a concentration camp but survived.

Polanski now had this other tragedy in his life, so he returned and began to investigate his friends who were in the entertainment industry. One interesting twist is that he thought at the beginning that maybe John Phillips of the Mamas and Papas might have been responsible for Sharon's murder. Why did he think that?

Polanski once had a speedy affair with Michelle Phillips, the wife of John Phillips, in London. He assumed that maybe John Phillips discovered this and, in a wild act of revenge, arranged for the murder of Sharon.

Polanski spent the first two or three months after his return playing detective. He went to John Phillips' house and borrowed equipment from the police department so that he could search for blood stains. He also checked Phillips' car for any weapons, but he found nothing, of course. It was all in his mind.

Poor Polanski was tortured and is still tortured. So, the Polanski story was a sad one. One thing that people don't know is that Manson killed or arranged for the murders of all the people that we know were murdered, but there were other collateral damage victims in this awful case, including Terry Melcher and Dennis Wilson. The fallout continues to this very day for those who were affected and have somehow survived.

HOM: Are there still followers of Manson? I've also heard that there's still a Manson Family even today. Is that correct?

Davis: Yes, there are still some devotees. And the reason I know that is even though I never went to Charles Manson's funeral in 2017, I know that Sandra Good and Squeaky (Lynette Alice) Fromme, who are some of the most loyal devotees of Manson, even today, went to see Manson in the coffin before he was cremated, and went to the funeral.

At the funeral, there were ten people. And this is pretty horrendous. But what happened after Manson was cremated? Instead of getting his ashes and throwing them into the river or mountains, many of the devotees got Charles Manson's ashes and covered their faces with the ashes. They also placed souvenirs into his coffin. So, it gives you some idea that there are still some loyalists hanging around on the parameters. They are older, certainly not wiser, but those who believe that Manson was innocent, as crazy as that sounds.

HOM: What do you know about the lawsuits now?

Davis: Even in death, the controversy over Manson continues. As you pointed out, all of a sudden, half a dozen claimants to the body, claimants to the possessions, whatever they were of Manson, all came out of the woodwork.

After a long six-month battle in court, Jason Freeman Manson, who is the grandson of Charles Manson, got the body and all of his possessions. The judge ruled out all of these other people. The amazing thing was that they all fought over Charles Manson's body. Jason, who had a ministry and believed that his grandfather was innocent, got the body and then had the burial. The interment and the cremation then gave a lot of his stuff to a museum, which is like a wax museum or a horror museum in Las Vegas.

By the way, the grandson of Charles Manson, Jason, had a father called Charles Manson Jr., and Manson Jr. had changed his name to get rid of the Manson name. But he could not ever shake off the fact that he was Manson's son. Then, when he was in his forties, he killed himself.

HOM: Manson's grandson was going to be on the show until he wanted us to pay him $1,000, so that didn't happen.

Davis: I think that he never knew his father or grandfather very well. Does he have to pay for the sins of his grandfather? You have to feel sorry for them. I'll tell you one other nibble. I had a book launch in Beverly Hills at the home of a writer about a month ago. The owner of the house invited a documentary filmmaker to attend.

The host of the party called me and asked if I had seen the guest list. I said that I had gone through it, and there was a guy named Michael Bruner. Do you know who he is? The owner of the house said, "No, I don't know who he is." I then told him that Michael Bruner was Charles Manson's son.

When I told him that Charles Manson's son was going to come to a party at his house, which is around the corner from Cielo Drive, he freaked out. He then got on the phone and disinvited Michael Bruner. It would have been interesting to see Michael Bruner because I think he's another young man who spent most of his life without knowing his father. Mary Bruno was his mother. A completely different family adopted him. Now, fifty years later, he learns who his birth father is.

I think it would have been interesting to talk to Mr. Bruner. But he wouldn't have known his father, so it would have been an unfair sort of almost hijacking at my book launch. But you've got to understand that the interesting thing is that the host freaked out when he thought, "I didn't want Charles Manson's son in my house." So, there are offspring of Manson around, and many of them don't know the true depravity of either their father or grandfather.

HOM: Yes, it's got to be very difficult to be a Family member of someone like Charles Manson because you get shunned like that even though you had nothing to do with the crime. Now the House on Cielo Drive, where the murders took place, is gone, correct?

Davis: Yes, that's correct. The house on Cielo Drive was eventually torn down by its owners, and they relocated to a new address. The other interesting thing is that the house of Waverly Drive, which Lino and Rosemary LaBianca owned, and where they were murdered, is still there. It was just sold for about two and a half million dollars to someone who is maybe going to turn it into a museum.

HOM: At the end of the book, what is it you hope that readers will take away from it?

Davis: I found that a lot of young people don't know that Manson was the monster that he was. Over twenty to twenty-five years, and if you look back, you can see Manson performing on primetime television. You can see Manson perform this brilliant theatrical act of the monster in captivity, and Manson loved those little performances. Manson was theatrical. So, the point, I guess, is that many young people born after the year 2000 probably think that Manson was okay.

I was in Seattle visiting my daughter when two young men came in to remodel her kitchen. And when we started talking about crime, and I asked them about Manson, they both said that he was the guy who wanted to clean up our environment. He wanted clean water, and they both thought that he was okay because he had never killed anybody. I thought to myself that if these men, at the age of thirty, believe that, then obviously, their memories are a bit fuzzy. But it's true that if you talk to young people today, they don't think that Manson was as guilty as he was. They don't know the facts. So, in a way, this is my excuse to get it out of my system.

Listen to the full interview with Ivor Davis on my website:

https://www.alanrwarren.com/
house-of-mystery-episodes/
episode/b886018e/manson-
exposed-ivor-davis

Interview with Tom O'Neill

Tom O'Neill is an entertainment journalist whose articles have been published in national publications, including *Us, Premiere,* and *The Village Voice.* He wrote a book called *Chaos: Charles Manson, the CIA, and the Secret History of the Sixties.*

We had a chance to interview Tom in 2019.

HOM: That's a massive connection that you have written about between the CIA and Charles Manson. Where does that come from?

Tom: It's complicated, and it took quite some time. I have a circumstantial case where Manson intersected with the CIA researchers in 1967 at the Haight Ashbury Free Medical Clinic, who were doing secret drug research to try to obtain hypno-programmed assassins' couriers, and they were using unwitting subjects. All that information that came out in congressional hearings in the mid-1970s was reported on.

One of the researchers denied being part of this program. His name was Louis Jolyon West, and he was at the clinic at the same time Manson was there for three months. West, for twenty years, had been trying to create precisely what Manson somehow developed the technology to do, which was to create hypno-programmed assassins. People who were described by experts and other witnesses at trial seemed like brainwashed zombies who did Manson's bidding. Including killing strangers just because they were told to by Manson.

HOM: So, do you believe that Manson used the same technique that agents from the West were using? Or was Manson taught how to do it by someone?

Tom: I don't like to say what I think might have happened. I only want to say that I know what happened. And what I know happened was that there was a doctor who was trying to learn how to do this. He had contact with Manson at this clinic when Manson was sent there by his parole officer, and he was also simultaneously researching drugs and violence.

During that period, Manson somehow managed to relearn how to do this again. I want readers to reach their conclusions as to whether they think it happened. That's why I began by saying I'm presenting a circumstantial case because I have no direct evidence that this doctor programmed Manson, programmed the women, or taught Manson any of that. I am simply stating that was the objective of his research. It had never been reported before that he had been working out of the clinic at the very same time Manson was visiting it every single day for two months. During that period, Manson evolved from a barely literate ex-con into a guru and the kind of hippie cult leader that we all recall today. He passed away a couple of years ago.

I'm presenting a case. I think there's a lot of solid evidence that something untoward happened. Bugliosi, the prosecutor who wrote the book *Helter Skelter*, says in the epilogue of his book that the biggest mystery of all to him was how Manson gained the knowledge to create programmed killers who would not only kill on command but without any remorse and with gusto, glee, and brutality. He also says in his book, and I quote it in mine, "Is it something he picked up in prison? Is it something he picked up out in the street? Is it something he learned from others?" That was the launching point for a massive part of my book.

HOM: How was this book to work on when you are dealing with Bugliosi and Hollywood? Were people very open to you when you were doing your research with them?

Tom: No, not at all. That's why it took twenty years, because, in the very beginning, when it was just a magazine assignment, I was trying to find an angle. They wanted me to tell a story commemorating what would have been the thirtieth anniversary of these crimes, which was 1999. My signing editor advised me to focus on the impact of the crimes on Hollywood, the culture, the relationship between stars and fans, and the stars' connection to their community in Hollywood.

I was not interested in that, and I dug pretty deep, starting to find contradictions in what was presented in the trial and later in the prosecutor's book about the official narrative of the case. I began exploring those contradictions and trying to determine what had happened. I heard a lot of this in interviews I conducted with key individuals in the case. You know, witnesses who had testified at the trial but had never spoken publicly before, people who had been in the Manson Family, and people who were associated with them. I interviewed friends and relatives of the victims. It was challenging to get anyone to talk at first, and it required considerable perseverance.

Then, once I started hearing things that supported the information I was accumulating, I thought I needed to find corroborating documents, such as reports that had been done at the same time the investigation was ongoing. That took a long time to access the Los Angeles district attorney's files and the sheriff's files. This was quite an accomplishment, as nobody had seen these before. A few researchers accessed some of the case files, but not all of them. However, nobody had seen the sheriff's files.

HOM: Did you get a chance to interview Charles Manson himself?

TOM: Yes. I interviewed him in 2000, but unfortunately, he wasn't allowed to have in-person visitors at the time. The majority of the time that he was in prison for all the years, at least since the Tate-LaBianca conviction, which was the first murder that he was convicted of, he was constantly in and out of solitary, or what they call the hole. He famously challenged authority, sought to disrupt the system, misbehaved, and I don't think he truly wanted to be among the general population. So, when he was in solitary confinement, he couldn't have visitors. He still had limited phone privileges, and I think maybe one or two nights a week, he was allowed to use the phone at nighttime.

So, my interviews were all conducted over the phone, which is frustrating when dealing with someone like him. If you've seen any of the videotaped interviews, it's hard enough to get a straight answer out of him, and he often plays games, answering in riddles, nonsense, and non-sequiturs. Also, anytime I would try to challenge him and press him on the phone, he had a guy (named Pin

Cushion) inside prison with him who was sitting there on the phone with him, and if Manson would get upset, he would hand the phone to this guy, who was kind of like his bodyguard in prison and his aid. This guy would yell at me and try to negotiate a different line of questioning. It was a frustrating experience, and I never had the opportunity to sit down with him face-to-face. Not that I think that I would have gotten any more, but I think I would have had a better chance.

HOM: In a few of the articles I have read, you have alluded to the fact that Manson himself didn't have a mental illness and that it was all an act. Is that correct?

TOM: Yeah, I'm pretty convinced of that because of his people. And when I say people, you know, he had a whole network of people inside prison and outside prison who supported him and handled his interview requests, mail, and donations. The main guy on the outside of the jail for most of that time was a guy called "Gray Wolf." When we were setting up the interviews, I informed Gray Wolf of what I wanted to discuss with Manson and assured him that I would provide Manson with any necessary funds, even though they were seeking payment. I said that I can't do that.

At one point, he played me a tape recording of himself describing my motivation as I had described it to him, Gray Wolf. He then explained it to Manson, and Manson began asking him questions about what he knew or what he might ask. He sounded completely coherent and not like Charlie Manson, the public Charlie Manson we all know. This was, I think, the real Charlie Manson. So, I'm sure there was some mental illness involved there, but not to the degree that everyone believes. I think he was playing a game, playing a character.

HOM: I've always thought that as well. What are your thoughts when it comes to the Beatles' *White Album* and songs like "Helter Skelter?" Do you think he believed that those songs were messages meant for him?

TOM: In the prosecution's theory for the murders, Manson wanted to ignite a race war that he thought was coming but was taking too long to happen. He called it "Helter Skelter," where he felt that ultimately, the Blacks were going to rise against the whites and to be this kind of apocalyptic race war that would end with all the Whites on the planet Earth being wiped out. Manson had promised his followers that he would hide them in this bottomless pit in the desert, where they would exist on rivers of honey and juice and feast on trees with candy and all manner of other delights.

Once the Blacks had wiped out the Whites, Manson said they would emerge from their hiding place and subjugate the Blacks and then start repopulating the planet with the perfect white offspring. So, I don't believe that Manson believed that for one second, but I think that many of the followers did— especially the younger women.

Bugliosi, I found out long after I'd interviewed him, so that I couldn't ask him about this myself. He'd said it twice in interviews—that he never believed Manson believed in it. But he was convinced that Manson's followers believed in it. I wanted to ask Bugliosi, but it was too late. He had already told me that he would never talk to me again and that he was going to sue me.

I wanted to ask him why Manson sent those people up there to start a race war and to try and frame the Black Panthers for the murders of Sharon Tate and the people who died with her at her house, and the next night, the LaBiancas. Why were they murdered if it wasn't for a race war? But Bugliosi went to his grave, so we were not going to know the answer to that, at least not from him.

HOM: It seems that you had a problematic relationship with Bugliosi. What caused that?

TOM: Basically, I had interviewed him very early, when it was still a magazine story, in the first month of my reporting. He was very generous with his time, and we talked all day. After conducting in-depth reporting, investigating, obtaining trial transcripts, and reviewing police reports, sheriff's reports, and DA reports, I found that a significant amount of information contradicted what he maintained had happened.

Once he found out what I was doing, he tried to impede my investigation. Ultimately, we had this very climatic, face-to-face showdown at his house six years after our first meeting, during which he shouted and yelled and cursed at me, threatened me, and said that my book was never going to be published because he would do everything he could do to stop it and that he was the best trial lawyer in the world. Unfortunately, he passed away before my book came out. I wanted him to be alive and accountable for all the stuff that is in my book, but that's not the case.

HOM: What can you tell us about what was going on in the Tate house? Numerous rumors are circulating. Can you set the record straight?

TOM: I wouldn't say that Sharon Tate was doing anything at all that should have resulted in her death or any of the other people's deaths, but there was a lot of stuff going on in the house in the six weeks or two months before the murders that Bugliosi hadn't reported. There were a lot of drugs, drug usage, and drug dealing and trafficking out of the house. There was a lot of violence going on in the house.

Sharon Tate and Roman Polanski left the house in March 1969. Roman went to London to work on a script and scout locations for a movie, *Day of the Dolphin*, as the director of the movie. Sharon went to Rome to make a movie. Sharon came back the day before the Moon landing, so July 19th. So, a lot of that happened before she returned home, but it was already known in

Hollywood as a place where such things were happening.

When Sharon got back, her friends told me that she was appalled and horrified by what she found out had been going on in their house. Abigail Folger and Charles Bukowski, who was one of Roman's friends, were all house-sitting and stayed with her even when she returned, despite being supposed to leave. Sharon didn't want them to stay, according to Joanne Petett (actress friend of Sharon Tate), who had a phone conversation with Sharon after she returned. She told her that Sharon was beseeching Roman to make them leave. She was crying on the phone to him, but he wanted them there for whatever reason. So, I don't know what Sharon saw or what occurred during the last three weeks of her life, but I have a pretty good idea that it was the same issues that were going on before she returned.

HOM: You were somewhat hard on law enforcement over the Manson case. What can you say about Law Enforcement during this case?

TOM: I wasn't as hard on them as Bugliosi was on them. He essentially called them fools and incompetent in his book, claiming that he had solved the case. They brought him information, and he put all the puzzle pieces together. He went out and initiated gathering evidence to support his theory, but they didn't take any action.

The reason they didn't do it was that they never believed his Helter-Skelter theory, and they also knew that he was making many things up. They didn't want to work that closely with him, fearing it would jeopardize their careers. They also, when I say them, it's pretty general, but the very highest at the LAPD and the sheriffs, I believe, but I can't say this definitively. Still, I present a fairly solid circumstantial case in the book, supported by documents and reports, that they knew what was going to happen before it happened and who was responsible when it happened.

Instead of immediately taking the Family into custody or even questioning them, they backed off. I'll leave it to your listeners to read the book and see why that happened and how it happened in the two or three months between the time of the murders and the time of the arrest of the Manson Family.

HOM: What has been the biggest surprise that you learned while writing the book?

TOM: From the responses I get from people who've read the book, who know a lot about the case before opening my book, I mean, there are a lot of people out there with an obsession with the case or, say, interest in the case, researchers, journalists, all kinds of people. What everyone seems to walk away with from my book, which is probably the easiest thing to be shocked by, is the fact that Terry Melcher, who was a pivotal person in explaining why Manson selected the house that Sharon lived in for the slaughter. The official narrative is that Terry, a rock and roll producer and the son of Doris Day, had rejected Manson. But he had led Manson to believe that he was going to record him, and then he didn't. The official version has Manson auditioning informally at the Spahn Ranch in late May 1969, and Terry telling Manson that he didn't think he could produce him, but suggested a friend of his who could come out and do some recording and possibly film for a documentary. Still, Melcher would have nothing to do with it.

However, what I discovered in the files and interviews from several different sources was that Melcher had a relationship that extended beyond the May audition. At trial, Melcher testified that he had never seen Manson again after that audition in May 1969, which was a couple of months before the murders. But what I found were documents, and in Bugliosi's handwriting, that showed Melcher had been meeting with Manson for several months after the murders and in theatrical situations at the Spahn Ranch, Barker Ranch, and Myers Ranch in Death Valley. Bugliosi concealed all of this from the defense, altering the narrative and ultimately leading to Terry Melcher's perjury on the stand.

This would have led the verdicts to be overturned, and still could be like Stephen Kay (co-prosecutor of the Manson murder cases), who looked at all of the documents I assembled and said this could lead to new trials. However, that hasn't happened yet. The books have been out for a couple of months now, and nobody has made any moves to do anything like that.

HOM: What about the possibility of any of the Manson Girls being released from prison?

TOM: If anybody's going to get out, it'll be Leslie Van Houton. She didn't participate in the murders the first night, the Tate murders. She was at the LaBianca house and was convicted of those murders. If you believe in parole, if you believe in rehabilitation, it's hard to make an argument for why she's still sitting behind bars. The parole committee has granted her parole three or four times now, and each time it reaches the Governor's desk, the Governor is the only one with the power to deny the parole committee's judgment. This has happened now for five or six years.

HOM: Why do you think that Bugliosi created such a narrative and changed things in the case for trial? Was it his thinking that this was the only way he could win the case?

TOM: I present a couple of competing theories in the book. One of them, and the easiest to believe, is that he had a book deal before the trial commenced, and he had a coauthor, Kurt Gentry, sitting in the front row of the trial every day, taking notes and working on the book with him. That would not be allowed today, and I'm surprised it was allowed then. The California bar has in its charter that you cannot be working on any commercial project associated with the case that's being processed. You may not be able to do it for several years until the case is brought to court. However, that's documented and proven. Both Kirk Gentry and Bugliosi even admitted to me that they were working on the book during the trial, which constitutes a conflict of interest. Bugliosi was interested in having as sensational a case as possible because that would sell more books. So, that's one theory as to why Bugliosi might have lied and presented a false narrative.

Another example is in the chapters later in the book, where you see what I discovered about Manson's parole officer and his catch-and-release policies, as well as the government programs that were operating simultaneously in the same year. It's possible that Bugliosi was answering to a higher authority who was saying this is how we need to prosecute this case.

HOM: Were you able to talk with any of the Manson Family?

TOM: Yeah, I talked to probably about eight or nine of them. Many of them wouldn't speak to me and adamantly refused my interview requests. I also showed up at the doors of several of them, and one or two of them called their attorneys. Many of them were living off the grid under different aliases. But I talked to Dianne Lake, Barbara Hoyt, Bruce Davis, Bobby Beausoleil, and Sherry Cooper. I have a list in the back of the book in the acknowledgments. I spoke with several of them.

Of course, the ones I wanted to talk to the most, who I think have the answers, were the ones who didn't speak to me. Tex Watson, Linda Kasabian, Nancy Pittman, and Danny DeCarlo are the individuals I believe are the secret keepers, those who know the what, the whys, and the what fors of this case and would be able to answer the questions I raised in the book.

HOM: What did they say about the race wars?

TOM: The ones I spoke to, like Dianne Lake, for instance, said she heard about it at least from the winter of '69 on, maybe earlier. And I do believe, like I said, that Manson was preaching that to them, but I don't think that Manson had the murders committed for the race war. I don't think that he ever believed it, and Bugliosi, who called himself the authority on the case, told *Rolling Stone* in

2015, before he died, and *Penthouse Magazine* in 1975, I think, that he never thought Manson believed in the race war motive for a second.

Listen to the full interview with Tom O'Neill on my website:

https://www.alanrwarren.com/ house-of-mystery-episodes/ episode/8018b23e/tom-oneill- charles-manson-the-cia

Interview with Mark Hewitt

In 2022, we had the opportunity to talk with true crime author Mark Hewitt, who had just released a book on Charles Manson titled *Charles Manson Behind Bars: The Crazy Antics and Amazing Revelations of America's Icon of Evil*.

The biggest thing that made this book and interview different was that Hewitt had written about Manson from the perspective of him living in prison. What was it like for Manson? Was he in solitary confinement all the time? Did he ever go out into the general population? This is something that hadn't been covered, at least not in a nonsensational way.

Often, when a television crew from a significant network entered the prison and conducted an interview with Manson, it created a whole new experience, which wasn't always entirely real. Manson ended up putting on a big performance for the cameras. The interviewer was also someone famous and had to try to make the interview exciting to keep people watching and talking about it. So, the questions were set up to help Manson create a show.

Knowing Hewitt's writing, which usually focused on the Zodiac Killer up to that point, I figured it would be a fairly level-headed and informative interview. I knew he would have some valuable information rather than just seeking the spotlight.

HOM: So, Mark, what got you into doing a book on Charles Manson, and not just the regular Manson-style book about the crimes that he was responsible for, but more following his life in prison?

Mark: I consider myself an actual crime author, but I backed into the whole area. It wasn't something that I was looking for. In 2004, I published a self-help book. I was a pastor and had written on the topic of change. During the process of promoting this book, I sought innovative and engaging ways to generate publicity. I spent some time thinking about who could benefit from a book on change and who could benefit from a self-help book.

The idea occurred to me that if I could get some high-profile individuals to read the book, it might generate some buzz. So, I wrote a number of letters to various high-profile individuals, including Charles Manson and some of the other big names who were alive and in prison. I had no idea what to expect, but before long, I was fishing letters out of my mailbox from Kenneth Bianchi, one of the Hillside Stranglers, to Arthur Shawcross, who is a serial killer of prostitutes in New Jersey.

One day, I pulled out a letter, and it was written in fourth-grade cursive. It had a swastika return address with a name I thought I'd made out to be Charles Manson. I was pretty surprised. But from that correspondence, I got to know him a little bit. I shared a little bit about myself with him, and he shared a little bit about himself with me. At one point, he mentioned he thought I was very optimistic. He noted that a friend of his who was incarcerated in the cell beside him was also a hopeful person. He called him Boxcar.

I didn't think very much of it, but maybe a year later, I got this letter from an inmate named Germo Mendez, who called himself Willie and said that he got my address from Charles Manson. When I wrote back to him, I asked him, "Your name isn't Boxcar, is it?" Sure enough, that's who it was.

Willie began sharing stories with me about Manson. I was pretty fascinated because these were stories that you wouldn't be able to get in the library from a published account. This was stuff that he had told me, like Manson said this, and Manson did this, or on one occasion, this is what happened behind bars. I was so fascinated by these that I kept asking for more. Then I said, "Willie, we ought to collaborate on a book together."

He was very excited about the idea and began writing page after page after page to me of all kinds of anecdotes, quotes, and stories from behind bars of his experiences with Charles Manson. The two of them grew quite close. They were real pals, and they would spend hours talking to each other between cells at night. They were each housed separately, had no roommates, and were alone. But they were next to each other and spent a lot of time talking.

So, that's how this book came about. Willie's the author of this book, if you want to put it that way. The pages and pages of information that he sent me, I was able to transcribe, edit, organize, and put together in book form.

HOM: Boxcar is a strange name. How did he get that name?

Hewitt: Well, his name is Willie, and Manson liked to name all his associates. He liked to give them nicknames, like all the members of the Manson Family were given nicknames, which is a cult tactic of stripping somebody of their identity. But Willie, the name reminded Manson of Boxcar Willie. Instead of calling him Boxcar Willie, he just called him Boxcar.

HOM: How did you feel about Boxcar? Do you think that he was pretty trustworthy and upfront with you?

Hewitt: Yes, but with a significant caveat. First of all, to be housed beside Charles Manson in prison, you don't get a traffic ticket, and you don't violate minor laws. This is a guy, I believe he told me that he was convicted of violating thirteen felonies, including armed robbery and attempted murder. He had also committed repeated violations in prison. So, he was a dangerous person.

He was a person with a very colorful and infamous background. In talking with me, he seemed to be very much on the level and very open and honest. I'm not gullible, and I'm not going to believe every word an inmate tells me. However, by and large, the things he told me did seem to corroborate the information I had obtained from other sources. He did strike me as a heartfelt person.

I think he does struggle with his impulse control. I suspect that early in life, he faced some complex challenges, and I believe he made many poor decisions. When push comes to shove, when anger rises or he gets frustrated, he knows what he's capable of.

However, as far as relating the facts to me, I felt very comfortable. I will say, though, that that's one of the weaknesses of the book: it's written by an inmate. All of the anecdotes and quotes come to us from him. So, his credibility is an issue. As well as anything that Manson says, you know, how credible is that? So, you have a bit of a broken telephone line between what's plausible and what's not. What's true, and what's not?

At the same time, what makes the book incredibly strong is that it is written from the inside. This is the only book about Charles Manson that has been written from the inside, from behind bars.

HOM: Was Boxcar, or Willie, ever worried about divulging personal information about Charles Manson from behind bars and then having it published in a book? Was Manson okay with this?

Hewitt: That's a question that I asked Willie over and over again as we put the book together because I was worried about his safety. I have heard and confirmed that Manson does not like having people write books about him. For whatever reason, it's probably because it's exploitative, or people get details wrong, or people make him out to be one thing or another. So, he does not want to talk to people who wish to write a book.

So, I regularly asked Willie, "Are you sure you want to publish this? Are you sure that you are comfortable with this?" Repeatedly, he told me, "No, no, no, it's okay." By the time we collaborated, Willie was in a different prison from Manson. He never expressed worry. What he told me was that he wanted to keep it real, to say the truth, to share his perspective, and to convey what he saw. He knew that Manson would understand, even if he didn't agree with it or like it. He would know because he was being genuine.

He never tried to make Manson look horrible. He never wanted to make him look in a bad light. At the same time, he never wanted to glorify himself. He would talk a little bit about himself. Manson had made an impression on him, and Manson influenced him in many ways. In his writing, I didn't get the sense that he was artificially elevating Manson, artificially trying to characterize him, or make him look bad. So, I can understand his opinion that if Manson read it, Manson would understand it, and I can buy that.

HOM: Now I have heard that Manson was abused when he was young and was even forced to wear a dress to go to school. What have you heard about that story or his childhood?

Hewitt: I guess it's a story that Charlie told Willie, and after writing it down, I found out that other people had heard that story too. So, it wasn't something Manson had said for the first time. Whether it's true or not, or if it's remembered by him differently than it happened, who knows? But it was a fascinating tale of him being punished. I guess a bully had picked on Manson, and he had gone home crying. And his foster father, of the family that he was staying with, I guess, was on the brutal side. He told Manson to stop crying and made him go back to school the next day wearing a dress so that he could show them that he was strong enough even to wear a dress to school.

HOM: Now, you mentioned Manson having a lot of wisdom. Was there something that Willie said to you that would make you think that Manson was wise?

Hewitt: No quotes come to mind at this time, but Charlie is a very philosophical thinker, quite a deep thinker. I've spent quite a bit of time trying to get my head around Manson's ideas because a lot of what he says seems to come from a variety of sources, including Christianity, Buddhism, other Eastern religions, and even mind control ideas. Hypnosis is something that he was very interested in.

So, Charlie essentially picked and chose from all these ideas and influences. So, his philosophy is composed of an eclectic mix from various sources. At best, there may have been a core to it. He's a profound thinker who cares deeply about the environment and is keenly aware of the corruption in society. I think it's worse.

Manson tends to pick and choose, using whatever is helpful to him. He's very skilled at taking advantage of others. I think he selects his ideas and philosophies to take advantage of people based on their needs, insecurities, or wants. I think the genius of Manson is that he's able to size up other people very quickly and manipulate them or bully them or do whatever he needs to do to get what he can get.

HOM: Now, listeners will want me to ask, did you hear anything about the Sharon Tate murders? Like about him not being there, or that he was set up and had nothing to do with the murders?

Hewitt: I did. They did broach that subject during some of the late-night calls and talks. Willie shared some of that with me, and there is a section in the book about those murders.

To this day, Charlie doesn't take responsibility for them and says he has nothing to do with them. A theory floating around is that Manson was helping his young people, and some of them went out and did them on their own accord. He kind of embarrassed Manson and blamed him for being the group leader and being responsible for these actions, when they were the actions of people who were associated with Manson.

I think that it's a hard way of looking at it from this point, from what we know about the situation. More recently, the understanding is that with the Tate killings, he sent them out there and told them where to go. He wasn't specific about what he told them to do, but the inference was clear.

More recently, it's come out that Manson went back to the Sharon Tate residence after the murders and participated in a certain amount of, I don't know if it was clean-up or checking out to see what was done, but he was there after the killing and before the police were notified.

Then, the next night at LaBianca's, it's pretty clear from all the sources that Manson was there first, and he was the one who tied them up before leaving and instructing the others what to do. Everybody knew that the two were going to be killed, and that's precisely what Manson wanted.

However, in discussions with Willie, he was able to shift the responsibility to them. He said he believed that the young people were trying to help somebody else who was already in prison and to do a copycat murder that looked similar to a previous murder, and that if this happened, the person in prison would be released because he didn't commit this murder.

HOM: I take it that Manson never expressed any regret that the Tate and LaBianca were murdered, even if by some of his followers, and he had nothing to do with it?

Hewitt: Yeah, and the whole theory of Helter Skelter and Manson trying to initiate a race war, that's also challenged by Manson and a lot of his followers. They say that Vincent Bugliosi got it completely wrong in his book *Helter Skelter*, and that there was no race war and no underlying philosophy. That's hard to believe as well because I think it's been well-documented that that's what Manson was attempting to do.

It's pretty possible that Manson got in over his head. He led this band of hippies, promoted counter-culture attitudes, and talked about a race war. When no race war happened, to remain their leader, he had to show that what he was saying was true. There may have been a kind of events set in motion that Manson felt trapped into that he had to try and make this race war happen because the young people were starting to doubt him. That's entirely possible.

I think that's one of the theories that Willie came up with, that maybe it wasn't premeditated, as far as Manson was such a horrible person that he intended to kill a lot of people. Still, perhaps he felt like he had to keep the respect of the people that he was trying to lead.

HOM: What did you learn about life in prison for Manson? Did he get along with other prisoners? Is he popular, or are others scared of him? How does he do with prison guards and authority?

Hewitt: I learned a lot about life behind bars.

There are three things that you do not do behind bars. One is that you do not disrespect another inmate. They thrive on mutual respect and respect for themselves. If there is a violation of this, then you can expect to be punished swiftly and severely.

Second, you don't insult an inmate's mother. That's something that every inmate holds very sacred. So, if you want to pick a fight, you mention something about somebody else's mother.

The third thing is that everybody's cell is their home, and it's treated with great care and respect. If you violate someone else's space or you violate somebody else's cell or their belongings in their cell, you risk being attacked or killed. These inmates behind bars have so little, the little that they do have, their self-respect, and their mothers, and their cells are guarded with great ferocity.

What was also interesting for me to find out about was the communication between inmates in a prison block. I suppose every prisoner has a fish line. It is a weight with a string attached to it, and they use it to throw to another cell, to pass notes along, or to pass possessions, such as a bag of potato chips or something similar. These prison cells are filled with lines being thrown back and forth and items being transferred from one cell to another. I thought that was very interesting, and Willie went into great detail about how all that worked behind bars.

Also, the means of wheeling messages. You can send messages from one end of the tier to the other end of the tier simply by announcing that you have a message to pass on, who the message is from, and who the message is to. If the person at the far end can't hear, then it will be relayed by a couple of the other prisoners who will listen to the message and then shout it and pass it on. It's almost like a verbal email system.

HOM: I would imagine that anyone else who is in prison with Charles Manson is probably also in for life as well.

Hewitt: Yes. Charles Manson is housed in Building Four in Corcoran, and it's a highly protected facility. Even with lifers, these individuals are under extra protection. It's a segregated housing unit, which means there are more guards, more locks, and more protection for them. That's because these are inmates who have committed particularly heinous acts, or they pose an extreme escape risk. Charles Manson is a high-profile person.

Willie was in building four because he had left his prison gang. When you leave a gang, I understand that you are a marked person. You were involved with a ruthless gang, and when you left it, there were death threats. That's why he ended up next to Charles Manson.

HOM: How does Manson get along with the guards? Are they specifically targeting him, or do they have to do something different because it's Manson? Or does he just get treated like the rest of the prisoners?

Hewitt: The guards are very professional. If they are not, they will run into trouble with the inmates. All guards are very professional in their approach, and they, too, must treat the inmates with respect. If they don't, they run into trouble with inmates who refuse to cooperate with them. Therefore, a certain level of professional relationship exists between the guard and the prisoner. For the most part, this is a countrywide issue.

Manson, in particular, is a very manipulative person who has been known to manipulate corrections officers into doing things for him.

Willie felt that when he was out with Manson for a couple of months, the guards were conspiring against him and doing things to annoy him. Willie suspected that Manson was behind it. Such as getting the shower turned off early or not getting all the food that he was supposed to get at lunchtime. He felt that Manson was probably pulling some strings. Willie believed that staff transfers were made as a result of either a conflict with Manson or Manson pulling strings and causing things to happen.

When Willie became very close to Manson, Willie noticed that people treated him differently. Correctional officers treated him differently. Other prisoners treated him differently because they realized that he was very close to Manson. In one respect, they were probably a little afraid of Willie, and in another, they were a little in awe of him for having these late-night talks with Manson and hearing a lot of inside information.

HOM: Did you get the impression that Manson is as clever as he appears in interviews? You know, very controlled, he knows the right thing to say to scare people, to get his points across. He always seems to be together. Is he that smart?

Hewitt: I think he's very crafty. He's very wily. He doesn't have a lot of education. It wasn't until later in life that he learned to read and write while he was incarcerated. He had severe problems. He couldn't even write a letter, which he could do now.

However, I think that a lot of Manson's smarts stems from street smarts. He feels insecure about not having extensive book knowledge, but he is very skilled at working with others. He knows how to size up others and knows how to get what he wants. He quickly identifies the weaknesses and insecurities of others.

That's how he built his Manson Family back in the sixties. He made contact with hundreds of people, but only a handful were willing to follow him and accept him as their guru. You know, it's not that he has this power over everybody, but he's able to find weaknesses in some people and make them do what he wants them to do. So, I think he's very intelligent.

I think he also deals with a variety of mental illnesses, and those have been documented. The older he gets, the more his vision becomes clouded by what's going on, what's real, and what's happening. I posted an audio of Manson, which was recorded within the last couple of months, and it was interesting to hear him speak because he still uses the language of the 1960s and thinks about some of the issues that were significant back then. At the same time, he seems to be growing increasingly distant from reality and becoming somewhat muddled in his thinking. He has been identified behind bars as someone with some mental health issues.

HOM: Does he still put on shows? Is he all full of rage like he is on television interviews, or is he a different person there, calmer and more rational? What have you heard?

Hewitt: I couldn't say today. But Willie told me a couple of stories from when he was housed beside him a decade ago. He noted that Manson would get very rageful, and he would yell, and he would scream, and he would go on about whatever grievance he had. He even held many trials in his voice, shouting above the sound of the tier, convincing this person or that group of any wrong that he ever thought of. There were times when he was so enraged and screaming so loudly that everyone else would just shut up and let him talk, hoping that he would burn himself out soon. That's kind of how everyone treated him at the time.

He was also very good at using other inmates to do the same. I don't know, probably for his amusement, but he would tell other inmates, "You do this, and we're going to do this, and we're going to play this prank on the guards by doing this." The inmates would cooperate with him and pull off some interesting stunts or simply engage in bizarre yelling, which would leave people wondering what they were doing. But the whole time, Charlie was in charge and doing it for his amusement.

HOM: Quite the character. Wasn't he going to get married soon to a woman named Star?

Hewitt: Yes, that was a couple of years ago. His girlfriend got a marriage license, but they never got married. When Charlie was asked about it later, Charlie said that it was just publicity. Then it came out, sometime after that, the woman who was going to marry him, the only thing she wanted was to get Charlie Manson's body once he died. She would be able to take possession of it as his wife, and she also wanted his artwork and music, and who knows what else. Manson knows how to get publicity, that's for sure.

HOM: Did you learn anything surprising or that you never knew before?

Hewitt: I found the whole case interesting, as I didn't know much about the case. I read the book *Helter Skelter*, the biggest-selling true crime book ever. I think it sold about seven million copies. It gives you a kind of insight into who Charlie Manson is and what happened back in the sixties. However, I think hearing some of these stories more recently has fascinated me. Sometimes, when people talk about Charlie Manson, they're talking about a character of his, an evil person. Some of his followers talk about him as being all good, brilliant, and inspiring. I think the truth is somewhere in the middle.

What interested me the most was learning about his childhood and how it affected him in his later years, shaping who he became. By the time Manson was released from prison, just before the whole Helter-Skelter thing, Manson had spent about half of his life either behind bars or in a group home or a youth advisory situation. He was confined a lot because they figured him incorrigible.

He faced some challenges as a child, having a challenging childhood. You mix that with a lot of abuse he took either while being incarcerated or confined as a child. That, combined with his small stature, makes him a very petite man. I think he's only about five feet two, and he's never been very big or bulky. You mix all that, and you get a very fascinating person.

HOM: Did you find out if he had any sexual relationship with any other prisoner?

Hewitt: Manson is in his eighties now, so a sexual relationship is not really at the forefront of his mind or biology by this point. There are a few things in the book about his sexuality that I'd rather not get into at this point. But some of the conversations that Manson had with Willie were insightful and eye-opening, so let's leave it at that. But that brings up another interesting point that I learned about Manson: that he could spend months at a time in his cell without ever coming out or having anyone else in.

Part of that, I think, was his paranoia and being scared of other people. And to some degree, rightly so. Anybody who kills Manson today, and several inmates have tried to kill Manson, so he is a targeted person. So he's afraid of everyone. He's scared of the guards and other inmates. He doesn't know whom he can trust. Trust has been an issue in his whole life. He's never had somebody in his life whom he could put his trust in, so he's learned to distrust other people. As a result, he has spent a year in prison without ever coming out of his cell. That's quite unusual, as most inmates look forward to the time that they can go outside, walk around, talk to other people, and get some relief from their incarceration in a tiny cell. But Manson is quite pleased to stay in his cell and not go out.

HOM: That is true. He would have to be cautious, as someone could try to kill him. Like Dahmer or other high-profile prisoners, the killer would make a name for themselves by killing Manson. How long were Willie and Manson in prison, being housed side by side?

Hewitt: A little bit more than a year. For a couple of periods, they were at odds and didn't talk to each other. But they always made up and continued to communicate. Everyone around them knew that a special relationship existed between the two of them because they spent a great deal of time together.

HOM: Willie has been moved to a different prison?

Hewitt: Yes, he's constantly being moved around. I suppose he gets upset with something or disagrees with something, and he presses for a transfer to a different prison. There's talk that he might get paroled soon because of the overcrowding in the California prison system. Many inmates are being released. I find it difficult to believe that they would release somebody with as many felonies as Willie. However, he feels confident that he will be granted parole so that you may see him back on the streets again.

HOM: How old is Willie now?

Hewitt: He's in his mid-forties now. He's got a lot of life left. That may also be why Manson was comfortable with him because Willie was much younger, and Manson felt that he could probably manipulate Willie. And perhaps he did. At least at the beginning, Willie looked up to Manson and came to believe that he was a great person who possessed a great deal of wisdom and could genuinely help him. Later, he began to doubt his initial thoughts.

HOM: Are you still in contact with Willie?

Hewitt: Yes, we correspond regularly, and he continues to share information that he gets about Manson. Obviously, at a distance, but when he hears something, he tells me.

HOM: Maybe when he gets released, you can meet with him? Have you met him in person before?

Hewitt: No, I haven't met him in person, but he says when he gets out, he'd like to take me fishing and camping.

Listen to the full interview with Mark Hewitt on my website:

https://www.alanrwarren.com/
house-of-mystery-episodes/
episode/a96e7d81/mark-
hewitt-charles-manson-behind-
bars

Interview with Dary Matera

Dary Matera was a reporter for the *Miami News* for five years after he graduated from the University of Miami in 1977. He covered a wide range of topics, including crime, politics, and education. In 1986, he began writing nonfiction and true crime stories, becoming an author. At the time of this interview, in the Spring of 2016, Matera had nine books published.

The book we interviewed Matera about for the show was named *Charles Manson: Conversations with a Killer, Manson's Life Behind Bars*. Like the previous interview, the details of the book center on Manson's life while in prison. This time, the information for the book came from Edward George, who was Manson's longtime prison administrator and counselor. He also helped out with publicity for Manson.

Matera had far more insight into whether Manson was still actively pursuing people who were living outside of prison and maybe even having them murdered.

HOM: You had initially published this book back in 1999. What can we get from this book?

Dary: It picks up where *Helter Skelter* ends. The last chapter of *Helter Skelter* is the first chapter of my book. It's such a segway that Vincent Bugliosi, who wrote *Helter Skelter*, is endorsing my book right on the front cover.

HOM: So, what made you write this book?

Dary: Well, similar to the John Dillinger book that I wrote, someone who had a manuscript, a nonprofessional writer, actually the counselor and prison administrator, had a manuscript about all of the famous prisoners that he encountered in his life working at California prisons like San Quenton, Sing Sing, and the Vacaville State Mental Institution where Manson was.

He had a manuscript that needed polishing, and he went to my agent, who told me to work with this guy. I knocked out a book. Then the publisher decided to throw out all of these serial killers from the book, Sirhan Sirhan, the Green Mountain Killer, and the Black Panthers, and they wanted the book to be totally about Charles Manson.

HOM: This was taken from the prison counselor?

Dary: Yes, it was a prison counselor. A fascinating story. He was an Air Force pilot who became a seminary student. He went five years to become a priest and then couldn't deal with celibacy. So instead, he became a counselor. That was his priestly duty while he could still have sex and a family and wouldn't have to pretend to be celibate. His name was Edward George, and he was now almost ninety years old. He was Manson's counselor and later his friend for the last thirty years.

HOM: That must have been interesting, and how were his stories about counseling Charles Manson? Wouldn't that have been a scary job?

Dary: Yes, very scary. The book opens with Ed's first encounter. Ed was a priest accustomed to dealing with difficult people, having served in the military. He was a big, tall man, so he wasn't a shrinking violet. But in his first encounter with Charles Manson, he wasn't even warned. Edward was walking down a dark corridor in one of these prisons after sundown, and the next thing he knew, a little troll monster was playing head games with him. It wasn't even five minutes in, and he realized that it was Charles Manson.

That's how the book opens, and it begins this long, complicated relationship between the two of them. Manson is a truly fascinating individual. Had he not been a killer, he could have channeled his abilities in other areas. He would have been famous, perhaps as a rock star, a cult leader, or a preacher, or something like that. He was a mesmerizing character.

It almost destroyed Ed George, the priest and counselor. Manson got in his head, and he had his wild period where he left his wife and family, bought a motorcycle, and wanted to live the sex, drugs, and rock and roll Charles Manson's life. It's a remarkable story.

HOM: That's what was coming to my mind. That must have been quite a challenge for a counselor, as you're up against Charles Manson. He is very smart with a lot of charisma and knows how to manipulate.

Dary: Their relationship was such that Manson was never in chains or locked down. They would sit in Ed's office and shoot the breeze. They got to be that close. Then, when other visitors arrived, they would allow media interviews, and Charlie would become agitated and sometimes even attack the reporters or Ed. Then Ed would say to him, "Charlie, why did you have to do that?" Then, the next day, Charlie was sitting in the room with Ed, free as a bird, never having attacked Ed.

HOM: What was it about Charlie? Why would Ed George, the counselor, actually be friends with Charlie now? That I don't quite understand. I see when it's your job, and you are his counselor, and you are doing your job. But now, being friends?

Dary: Yes. You know relationships happen. Under any circumstances, why do women beg horrible serial killers to marry them? You see that all the time. Some famous serial killers are receiving love letters from fans and women who have read their stories and seen their pictures, forming these relationships.

Ed had formed this relationship with Charlie over ten or fifteen years, during which time they had been together and responsible for each other. When he was hired, they said, "We got this lunatic Charles Manson. He's your problem, and you take care of him."

Ed got to know the Family members, and he also met the women who were still free. He got to know Squeaky Fromme, and Squeaky would frequently call Ed. He almost became a Family member. He was like one of the gang. So, the relationship was maintained.

When the book was released, Charlie was upset with Ed and yelled at him. They ended their relationship. After that, Ed liked to stay in touch and see how he's doing. Charlie is living forever; he won't die. He's in his seventies now, and everyone is still afraid of him.

HOM: Is Charlie still getting married to some twenty-five-year-old woman named Star?

Dary: Yes. Just as I said, why would Ed maintain a friendship with him? He's a prison counselor, and he's a priest. A priest is going to maintain a relationship with anybody that he's trying to save. That's their calling.

But prisoners have groupies. Charles Manson has this woman trying to marry him, and she's terrific. She's not some desperate woman. She's just a gothic kind of person. Her name is Star, a dark metal type who wants to be Mrs. Charles Manson. She was only in her twenties and ready to marry him, but she obtained the marriage license only to have it expire before they could tie the knot. She must have ticked him off somehow.

Squeaky must have cried, or Sandra Good, who had been free all these years. One of his main minions probably got to him. They probably all cried that he was marrying this little heartbeat. So, he didn't go through with the marriage.

HOM: There is a difference, as Ed had been around Manson for several years, but this girl had never met him, and yet she wanted to marry him.

Dary: Charles Manson, for the last thirty years, has gotten more mail than probably all the other prisoners in the entire prison system combined. He still gets bags of it. Ed George's responsibility was to screen Charles' mail. So, every psycho crazy "Marry me, I love you, I will kill for you, Charlie," and there are a lot of letters that say, "I will kill for you," too. Ed had to read them all. Bags and bags of mail from teenage kids who liked that whole cult ideal and environment.

HOM: Does Charlie still tell people what to do?

Dary: Charlie had a woman try to kill the president for him, and she would have succeeded if someone had taught her how to use a gun right. She got right in Gerald Ford's face, and without chambering the round, the gun didn't shoot. Charles Manson would have been responsible for killing a president. That was Squeaky Fromme.

HOM: How is it that Manson can capture and mesmerize so many people and get them to do so many bad things? We were not just talking about going into a store and stealing a pen or something. We are talking about murder. How can he do that?

Dary: He had great hair. No, well, he looked cool. He looked like Jim Morrison of the

Doors. He was cool, dark, and scary. He's the epitome of every teenage girl who likes the bad boys. You know, he's the "Fonz" times one hundred. Plus, he spoke very well and was mesmerizing, and he knew how to use drugs. When you get a young teenage girl high, and you start talking to her about uplifting herself and extending beyond who she is, don't listen to your old fogie parents. He had women who would do anything for him. They had sex with anybody to please him, and they were beautiful women.

HOM: Does Manson still have any Family alive, like parents or children?

Dary: Well, I don't know what happened to his stepfather, but his mother died young because she had drug issues (in 1973 at age 55 while living in Spokane, Washington). More intriguing is all the children that he is supposed to have had. Remember that Charlie had two or three years of sex every night with all of these young, fertile teenage girls, and they were popping babies in the clan a lot. There are Charles Manson juniors out there, but nobody wants to go by that name. They're all hiding the fact. You can see why.

HOM: What are your thoughts on whether Manson was ever at the murder scene at the Tate household, either during the murders or after they happened?

Dary: I see on the internet that there are people who don't know the whole story. Everyone claims that Manson was never there, but he was. He went afterward and cleaned up the scene. People often forget that others forget. People say that Manson never killed anybody or that he didn't commit any murders. Yes, he went to the house after the slaughter and tried to clean up the scene so that the CSI team would overlook his gang. So, he was there. The LaBianca murders, he went in first on the next day and tied them up. He told his gang to go in and slaughter them. So, he was at both houses.

HOM: I think one of his Family members is going to be released from prison on parole.

Dary: Well, they always say that one is going to get out. Here's the deal with the Manson Family. As horrific as the crime was, they are way beyond their expiration dates for prison sentences. The longest people in the whole prison system are people who have committed horrific crimes, and they get out in ten to fifteen years or less. The Manson Family has been in prison for almost fifty years. A half-century. All of these teenage girls, now in their seventies, still won't let them out because of the publicity. Our prison system is not based on who committed the most publicized crimes. The rehabilitation and parole system should not consider that. But of course, everything is celebrity and media in America.

So, those poor people can't get out. It's hard to say poor people, but if you're an eighteen-year-old on LSD and you're wandering around in a house, and you don't even know what you are seeing, it is real. You are now a seventy-two-year-old woman, and society still fears you. It's harsh.

There are ten thousand examples of people who have committed horrendous crimes and gotten out in one-third of the time, as the Manson Family. They let Susan Atkins out for a day before she died. She was one of the worst, though. She was the one who cut up Sharon Tate's baby. She was horrible. She wasn't going to get out, but she was dying of cancer.

HOM: Leslie Van Houten has been granted parole, but the Governor always rejects it.

Dary: He has in the past. I think Leslie has been granted parole in the past, and some of the others were granted parole, but Jerry Brown (the Governor at the time) stopped it. He's the worst governor to be in office for the Manson girls because he was around back in that era. Jerry Brown was the first hippie governor, so he feels mad about that.

Ed George, whom I wrote the book about, supports Van Houten's release. He's been saying since the book came out that she should be paroled, that she was young, and she didn't know what she was doing. But I bet they don't let her out. People are terrified, but what do they think? Even if you let Charles Manson out, what are they going to do, bring their walker?

That's just one side of the story. There are still all of the young people out there writing him letters who are willing to kill for him. He could start a new Family. But the old Family isn't going to do anything.

HOM: What is the thing that sticks out the most when you were talking with Edward and putting together the book? Were there any surprises for you?

Dary: Well, the thing that stood out the most was how close on the edge Manson could have come to being Jim Morrison or another rock star or being someone positive in history. How near he came to being a cult leader with a positive force, almost like Gandhi.

Without the prison influence, the power he had over recruiting people and getting them to do his will was so strong that he could have gone down in history as a good figure. Gandhi or Timothy Leary created LSD in the cult movement. He was a talented musician, able to write songs, so he was on track to become a rock star like Jim Morrison.

A second surprise was the story of Helter Skelter, which was that Manson did the killing so that he could create a Black White war, and that came out of Manson's prison life because there was huge segregation. There are so many African-American prisoners that they dominate the prison system. Manson was always trying to survive as a white guy. So, he had the idea that the Black people were going to take over the world. It's very doubtful that his murders were based on that. That just caught Vincent Bugliosi's attention, enabling him to prosecute the case.

The reality of the murders is that one of the guys was good-looking (Bobby Beausoleil), and all the girls liked him. He got busted. The Manson Family decided to do a copycat crime so that the cops would figure that it wasn't Beausoleil and let him go.

HOM: Do you think that Manson has been responsible for any deaths since he's been in prison?

Dary: Yes. The Manson Family Murders involved eight people. Manson has been responsible for at least thirty more deaths since he's been in prison, by just giving out orders or sending out messages, and killing old enemies and people he doesn't like. You were not going to hear about it because the American government is not going to let people know that imprisoning someone is not going to end their reign of horror.

If anyone challenges that, you just have to think that he almost got the President killed while he was in jail. So, he would have accomplished killing the president of the United States from his jail cell. The message was sent, and Ed George was right there. Squeaky Fromme, who had tried to shoot Ford, was calling Ed, begging to talk with Charlie. Finally, on Christmas, he let Squeaky speak to Charlie, and Charlie gave her some code to follow.

HOM: Any feeling about what Manson believed in for religion?

Dary: Manson is a spiritual person, but he always puts himself up as God. That was his thing. He claimed to be Jesus. He utilized his knowledge of religion to transform himself into a god-like figure, even surpassing that of a prophet. Manson wasn't going to be beholden to anyone. But as far as his own beliefs, I don't think he had anything beyond himself.

HOM: Do you think Manson will ever get out of prison?

Dary: No. Manson says he's like Frankenstein. If they let him out, the whole world will freak out, and they'll hunt him down. He is safer in prison. The villagers with the torches will appear anywhere he goes.

He doesn't even show up to most of his

parole hearings. When he does show up, he often has the swastika inked on his forehead. That doesn't appeal to the parole board.

HOM: What was Manson's appeal in using the swastika?

Dary: Mostly shock value. Showing you are anti-society. In the sixties, World War II wasn't that far away. It had only been about twenty-five years since the end of the war. So, what could an American rebellious person do to shock society the most was to wear a swastika. There was also that race war thing that Bugliosi claimed Manson was trying to start. For Manson to wear a swastika and to have his girls wear a swastika was like a signal for the Blacks to rise.

HOM: Why do you think Manson had Sharon Tate and the people at her house killed, as well as the LaBiancas? What was the reason for the murders?

Dary: There have been many theories. One of the theories was that he went to the house of Terry Melcher, who was Doris Day's son and a record producer. The Beach Boys had introduced Manson to Melcher. Manson wanted to be a rock star, and Terry Melcher blew him off because he didn't think that Manson was good enough. Manson then wanted revenge. So, they went to Melcher's house, but Melcher was no longer living there, fortunately for Melcher. His girlfriend at the time was actress Candice Bergen.

Another theory was that they had Redwood decks, and the Family comprised environmentalists who were enraged that they would cut down the Redwoods to make the decks.

A third theory was that Manson was familiar with the house from having been there. They had picked it randomly, and at the time, they had no idea who would be there. It turned out that a small party was going on. That was just random that Abigail Folger from the Folger coffee empire happened to be there. Manson had nothing against her. Jay Sebring was there. He was a Hollywood hairdresser. Manson had nothing personal against him. Even Sharon Tate or Roman Polanski had no personal animosity against them. They even killed the guy who was visiting someone at the guesthouse, who could have been a Manson follower. He was just a young kid. It was all about creating the scene, not who they murdered. It was about how the murders were done. What was written in blood on the wall, and how could they shock the world in this supposed Black-White war?

HOM: What were your thoughts on the Beatles' song "Helter Skelter" and if it had any influence on the crimes?

Dary: You've got to think of the drug culture of the time. They were doing a lot of LSD, marijuana, and other hallucinogenic drugs. So, if you're listening to the Beatles' *White Album* on LSD, you could be getting all kinds of signals coming from that music. But it was just about a ride at a fair. It was mostly the drugs that were frying their brain and making them hallucinate and read all this into it.

Listen to the full interview with Dary Matera on my website:

https://www.alanrwarren.com/
house-of-mystery-episodes/
episode/608a58d3/dary-
matera-charles-manson-
behind-bars

Interview with Simon Wells

Simon Wells, an English author, originally wrote and released the book *Charles Manson: Coming Down Fast* in January 2010. This is another one of the many great books to cover Manson and his Family. Like Jeff Guinn, Wells was great at capturing how the Manson Family lived their lives and gave one of the most accurate accounts of the crimes that they committed.

On a sad note, the author, Simon Wells, passed away from cancer in 2021. He was a wonderful person to talk to over the years, and he will be deeply missed. This interview took place in the Spring of 2016.

HOM: Can you explain the name of your book, *Coming Down Fast*?

Wells: There's a Beatles' song called "Helter Skelter," which I imagine your listeners know, which has got the line, "coming down fast." It's pretty much at the end of the song, "It's coming down fast, it's coming down fast," which was about a ride in London. We know that Helter Skelter was tied to the entire Manson mythology.

Helter Skelter is the title of Vincent Bugliosi's book, which is the prosecutor's version of the events, or his side of the story, told very well. I felt that there was another story to be told, not so much about the facts but how one approaches them. I think the thing is, with Manson, there's a lot of hysteria in the story. As someone who has been involved with many alternative communities, I wasn't too phased by that. I'm phased by murder, and I think everyone should be. But characters like Charles Manson were familiar, especially in California. There were many messiahs and creepy individuals who played to the people at the time.

To me, there was another reason for this, not the sort of spectacular semantics of Helter

Skelter, the prosecutor's interpretation of what Manson was saying about the race war and apocalypse. To me, it was a bit more mundane than that. So, I wanted to rationalize the whole story and bring it down to a level that was a little bit more understandable.

As a writer who is interested in the truth, the first thing that struck me when I heard about Charles Manson was that he was a serial killer or mass murderer who didn't kill anyone. The one murder that he is jointly associated with, it's possible, it's questionable, that had nothing to do with him as well.

So, there's a lot of madness tied to this story, and not just in the Manson corner—the hysteria from the prosecution angle, who wanted to make this a Hollywood nightmare.

HOM: They seemed to market Manson and his Family as what happens to your children if they become hippies. They turn into murderers.

Wells: Yes. However, there were many people like him in the hippie culture. I don't think he was special in that way. More people liked Timothy Leary at the time. The thing is, if he did control people, there wouldn't be many, and the people that he did control were all of a certain age. If they were around our age, they didn't take him very seriously.

One thing I discovered while researching this book is that many people came and went from Spahn Ranch. There was only an inner circle of about six or seven, and a hardcore of about a dozen. To me, this wasn't massive or the most dangerous man in America who's going to take over your kids. This is just a guy who influenced a small group of impressionable people. To honestly discuss the influence of cults, we can examine the case of Jim Jones. To me, I think that's a real cult influence, and I don't believe it's Manson.

HOM: How do you attribute their killing for Manson, then?

Wells: The infamy of the killings is down to Sharon Tate, period. If Sharon Tate had not been murdered there, we would not be talking about this today. I doubt anybody would be talking about Charles Manson. It was an attack on Hollywood. It was an attack on a celebrity, which exponentially elevated the case.

I traced the murder figures in L.A. in the sixties, and it's pretty shocking. Additionally, as part of the research, I checked on murders in places like Watts, where they might get one or two detectives assigned to them and be signed off in a couple of days. The Tate murders alone had a hundred detectives on them.

Then, of course, there's the prosecutor who did a brilliant job in making Manson, whose crimes were, as far as that's concerned, accessory and conspiratorial, into nine counts of first-degree murder. So, he did a fantastic job on that. What it did was create the monster that was Manson.

HOM: Was this why you wrote the book?

Wells: Yes. This was my brief. It was not to follow the Helter-Skelter route that Manson wanted to take, which was to go out into the desert and establish a tribe of millions, aiming to take over the world. Mine was to portray a small-time busker and a small-time criminal with influence over a specific group of people.

One of the reasons for the title *Coming Down Fast* was that I painstakingly traced the events leading up to August 8th and 9th, and what happened at Manson's commune and his self-proclaimed divinity. A series of events occurred in the run-up to the murders, which cast doubt on Manson's divinity, now in doubt among the commune. As he said himself in an interview, people were starting to question him. So, the last thing that he had left was to green-light these murders.

So, it's really about the collapse of a commune with a self-appointed messiah, so to speak, but the commune is breaking down. It's a pretty dismal tale. However, the infamy lies in the targets within the house on Cielo Drive—Sharon Tate, Roman Polanski, and they were on the way to becoming A-list celebrities. The story is incredible, but I don't think it's the one that the hysterical media want to talk about. Manson, of course, played the part quite well.

HOM: He did. He would consistently deliver an excellent performance in interviews with the media. You could sell that easily.

Wells: Yeah, he is what people wanted him to be. That's the interesting thing. He's got nothing to lose. He will be in jail for the rest of his life. Another thing I find interesting is that he did desire something. He wanted to have a recording contract, which is pretty evident from the information I sourced. He was seeking a musical career, and, in the run-up to the murders that followed, Manson was probably quite happy about being the most famous serial killer in the world by default.

HOM: While putting together your book, you had to interview several of the Manson Family members. How was that?

Wells: It was a little problematic. My approach was to demystify this completely. As I mentioned earlier, make it more of a human story rather than a spectacle. The people I spoke to seemed to warm up to that approach. However, some people wouldn't talk to me because they had been taken advantage of in the past. I believe there's a backstory to it. I'm sort of keen to find it. If you remove the hysteria, then you are left with the story.

I had to talk about the murders, or we wouldn't be talking now. But what caused those murders is for me, and from what I came across, it is in no way what has been presented. I don't think Manson wanted to rule the world and cause a race war. He may well have discussed something similar around the campfire, but as someone who has sat around campfires, people often talk nonsense.

What we're looking at is a frustrated artist who felt he had a break in the music industry in the sixties, but it didn't come to pass. I think history would have been different if he had been given a contract.

The thing is, I listened to all of his music in preparation for this, and anyone with access to YouTube can hear a lot of his music. One of the people who auditioned Manson at the time said to me that around the campfire, there were all the girls, swaying, and it was hypnotic. It was terrific. But put that on tape, and it's lost. It lost so much in translation.

That was the problem: they couldn't capture Manson around the fire. Terry Melcher, the individual who had to inform Manson that he wouldn't be getting a recording contract, had interesting plans to film Manson, thinking it would be a better way to present him.

If you listen to Manson now, I get the same feeling: it was okay, but only OK, and nothing earth-shattering. I think Manson had been detached from the real world during his prison stint. He didn't catch on to the hype of the music industry, whereas they would tell him that he was great and was going to get a music contract, and he believed it.

But I don't think there was any hidden conspiracy. I think if there were, it would have been sourced out very quickly. A lot of people have said that this was a drug hit, but from what I sourced out, the Manson Family really couldn't organize that much. The only drug hit that I came across was Tex Watson's attempt as a drug dealer, which was so sloppy that the mob wouldn't trust Manson and his clowns with a significant drug hit.

HOM: What was the thing that caused all of these murders, then?

Wells: Well, we had a succession of arrests within the Manson Family, starting with the death of an associate, Gary Hinman, in a biker drug deal that went wrong. It ended in his death by an associate of Manson, Bobby Beausoleil. There was also the beginning of questioning Manson's divinity. If there was suspicion of the pending race war, and it wasn't happening. Also, Manson's musical career wasn't happening.

The key for me was that he went, in the midst of all this, to a New Age institution called Esalen, which I believe is still located near Carmel, California. As a last-ditch attempt, remember that Terry Melcher and the Beach Boys rejected him in terms of his music career. He went to this place for a weekend, thinking they might enjoy his music, but they laughed him out.

So, Manson comes back to the ranch at about 2 o'clock after this rejection. Rejection ran large throughout Manson's life, from a small child, his parents, and rejection from society, which drove him toward becoming a criminal. So, the rejection is heavy.

When he got back to the ranch, the girls had cooked up this idea of one way to get Bobby Beausoleil out of jail, as he had been arrested for the murder of Gary Hinman, was to do a copycat murder by writing on the walls with blood, similar to what had been written on the wall during Hinman's murder. Manson just went with it and said to do it and make it grisly.

HOM: Why did they choose the Cielo Drive house with Sharon Tate?

Wells: Why did they choose Cielo Drive? I have a couple of ideas on that. There was the Terry Melcher connection, and he was the one who rejected Manson. He had moved away from that house. Manson's sort of prison sensibility led him to know that at the end of the drive was possibly the best place to do something like this. It was logistically a good plan.

Tex Watson, who was the principal hatchet man that night, had been extricated from the drug deal, and Manson had shot the dealer, believing that he was a Black Panther, so there was a debt there. So, Tex Watson was certainly under orders to repay that debt. Both Tex Watson and Susan Atkins had been doing speed and methamphetamines, so they were high as a kite and bouncing off the walls as far as I could find out. That was the reason for it. I've had no other indications of any other reason for it.

As I said, I don't think that they would have been trusted to do a drug hit for any of the motorbike gangs. I would like you to look at this academically and as dispassionately as possible. I can't imagine that any one of the Manson Family would have been trusted with relieving a large amount of drugs from the Tate house. There are rumors, and even police initially thought that it was a drug deal. They originally thought that's why it went off-target for a while.

HOM: Did Manson know Sharon Tate?

Wells: No, I don't think that they knew she was going to be there. Terry Melcher lived in the house, so it was going to be occupied by movie stars. Manson's instructions for that night were to go to others' homes as well, which, for whatever reason, they didn't. The fact that it is centered on one place makes me think that if there had been other houses on the same drive on the same night, then the story would have been different.

There is some suspicion that a phone call was made to the house to check and see if anyone was there. But from the information I got from the interviews I did, I think Charles Manson only met Sharon Tate once when he had gone to the house looking for Terry Melcher, but I doubt that he knew who she was. If he did, he also hung out and was a well-known face in the area, having probably seen many famous people. Again, I don't think he cared, and I don't think there was any planning involved. It was just a snap decision.

HOM: In your view, what was his relationship with the Beach Boys?

Wells: Dennis Wilson. Two of the girls were hitchhiking, and they met Dennis. Dennis used to cruise for girls anyway, so that wasn't unusual. The girls went back to his place with him, and when Dennis went to his recording studio, Wilson returned to find that the Manson Family had moved into his house. However, I think Dennis initially thought this was a large group of women who were obedient to whatever needed to happen. Manson was probably quite eccentric, but fabulous company, at least to start with. There's an interview in a British magazine called *Rave* where Dennis Wilson is extolling Manson's talent and saying that Manson was going to be recording for the Beach Boys label. I think Dennis got a little spooked later, but initially, it was a party.

HOM: How was Manson's younger life?

Wells: Unusual to perhaps normal society, but for those who follow the path of being a criminal, it was pretty predictable. You know, you had an unmarried teenage mother who tossed the kid around to aunts and grandmother, then fell into reform school living, and then junior prison. Remember, he wasn't a great criminal, as he was constantly being caught. This is not a mastermind. I think he was a result of what happens when a child is rejected early on and made to feel like an outsider.

HOM: What about the story going around about Manson's stepfather making him wear a dress to school one day?

Wells: Yes, again, this is not too unusual for children who are out of the ordinary and misbehave back in the day. We're talking about the nineteen thirties. So, it wasn't precisely in enlightened times. He was an outsider in school as well, so he did things that had an impact later in life when he was able to connect with young people. Because I think he understood what it was like to be an outsider. Remember, the Manson Family was not made up of women. They were all girls and were all outsiders in society then.

The other thing was that he was released in 1967, and he had spent half of his life in jail. So, you take sixteen years off his age when he was released, which was thirty-two. Therefore, he was probably still a teenager in his mind at the time.

HOM: Then what happened to him?

Wells: To me, I think that's when the story gets fascinating. He's thrown into the Summer of Love. Right into this incredible explosion of love, peace, drugs, and Manson is right in the thick of it. No wonder he was popular.

HOM: Really good timing!

Wells: I hate to say this, but it was impeccable timing. You know, if he'd been lucky with a record contract, we'd be talking about how he'd have been a Jim Morrison or John Lennon. He comes from humble beginnings and had a difficult childhood. I don't know about Jim Morrison, but John Lennon did. He had a difficult childhood, having lost his mother and father, and then went on to make a fortune as a rock and roller, inspiring everyone.

HOM: How did Manson feel about the Beatles?

Wells: Manson had a fascination with the Beatles. I think, in a sense, he saw himself as coming from humble beginnings and being able to make music that turned the world on. I think he saw it that way. He allied himself with the Beatles. He always used Beatles terms. When he had a bus, he called it the "Magical Mystery Tour." When the *White Album* was released, he was intrigued by it. The lyrics drew a connection between what they were saying and his movement.

HOM: Do you believe that Manson brainwashed his followers and had control over them? If so, does he still have control over them today?

Wells: That's a big question. Brainwashed them? I think he chose those who would do the murders. He knew that they would take to doing them. Interestingly, Squeaky Fromme, who one would assume was the absolute embodiment of Charles Manson, didn't go on it. So, that's interesting. Brainwashing was possible.

But the time was the time. There were many communes with self-appointed leaders whom people followed, not necessarily killed for. I think it's possible in the madness of the era, the madness of the time.

The other thing was that the time was the time. I think most young people now would Google him to see if he was on the same level. I think there was an innocence then.

But for actually hypnotizing and brainwashing them, I'm not so sure about that. I think they were convinced by what he had to say. He enthralled them, and maybe they believed him. Were they brainwashed, or were they like that anyway?

I think if he were demonic and evil at that point, they would have cleared out and found something better. There had to be love and attraction there. There had to be something. Perhaps loyalty, too. Maybe they were just loyal to the cause and believed in what he was saying. I think it's somewhere in the middle. It was something they were looking for, and it seemed plausible. We all believe in something. Does that mean we were brainwashed?

HOM: What about Manson's plans to hide his followers or Family from the world?

Wells: Manson wanted to detach his Family from the world. So, they didn't have watches, clocks, or days of the week. The time was supposed to disappear. It was intended to be an inclusive unit where they had limited contact with the outside world.

What they were listening to was Manson's music and his talk. They all shared in that. I think that inside themselves, they liked that. I find it interesting when you get some members of the Manson Family today saying that they regretted being there, but I don't think they did. They enjoyed it and appreciated the community aspect.

But let's be clear that the people that he sent out to murder had it in them to do that. I don't think anyone was forced to do that. In fact, on the second night of the murder, I believe Susan Atkins couldn't go through with it, and Linda Kasabian, who was the driver, couldn't do it. But she could drive. I think to go and kill someone, there has to be something inside of you to do it.

HOM: You also talk about another murder in London that is connected somehow. What was that?

Wells: It was a surprise on many levels. Sandra Good, who was in jail at the time of the Tate and LaBianca murders, was quite a vociferous convert at the time. She came from a well-to-do family in San Francisco. She had a boyfriend named Joe Pugh, and in the Manson Family's mythology, she was considered married to him by association. He went on a journey to London in 1969, and he was found in his hotel room with his throat slashed. And he also had cuts on his arms and all over his body. This was later called under suspicious circumstances, which is funny because I think if you found anyone with their throat slashed and they had marks all over their body, it would be suspicious.

It was also suspected that a very roving member of the Manson Family, Bruce Davis, was in Britain at the time, and it was suspected that he had a hand in this. This is how it's presented in the *Helter Skelter* book by Vincent Bugliosi, and it has become part of the mythology, gathering a lot of attention.

As a British-based author, I was intrigued by this story and felt compelled to investigate further, as I had never imagined Manson would have any connection to the United Kingdom. He was deeply rooted in Southern California, with its iconic Beach Boys and the vast deserts.

I went as deep as I could with the research into the death of Joe Pugh, and I discovered that he had an advanced mental health issue. He was very advanced when he was in London. The coroner here, when he was investigating it thoroughly, had concluded that the death was self-inflicted. Suicide is so rare that people cut their throats and slash their bodies in that way.

But what was interesting is that Bruce Davis was in the U.K. at the time. He may have been, and he may not have been. But I wanted to get to the bottom of this for one reason. Many deaths were attributed to the Manson Family if you read *Helter Skelter*. I think it's thirty, or at least the suspicion of thirty. But I think ultimately, Joe Pugh's death, as a suspected Family murder, was evoked to sort of ramp up the murder toll to make the Manson Family even more demonic than they seem to be. It just came to me that it was an unfortunate story that someone who was allied to one member of the Manson Family, whose relationship had ended way before, Joe Pugh, had never met Charles Manson before. He didn't know any of the Family members.

But the reality was that I think many people want to jump on the Manson bandwagon and evoke deaths all over the place to sort of give the story more horror. As far as I can tell from the murders attributed to the Manson Family, I will stress this: nobody's been convicted. There's only one, which was the death of a young man, his name was John

Haught, otherwise known as Jesus. He was found dead after playing Russian Roulette with a fully loaded revolver, with members of the Manson Family present.

We had stories about other bodies in the desert about five or six years ago, but that didn't come to anything. This was a celebrity case, and there were lawyers desperate to jump on the bandwagon to get their names in the story.

Interview with Jeff Guinn

We saved the best for last! In all of the years that I have been doing interviews with authors and have been watching documentaries or reading books on Charles Manson and the murders that he was behind in the late sixties, one of the best sources of accurate information has been Jeff Guinn.

If there is any true crime story you want to know about, I recommend first visiting Jeff's website or your preferred book source to see if he has covered the case you're interested in. You won't find anything better!

This interview is from the Fall of 2013, after Jeff released his book, *Manson: The Life and Times of Charles Manson,* which not only covers the murders but gives an in-depth history of Charles Manson himself, where he came from, who his parents were, and what kind of life he led.

HOM: Can you give us a short overview of the Charles Manson case?

GUINN: This all happened during the 1960s. Charles Manson slowly gathered together a group of followers that he called his "Family." Most of them had emotional problems and/or were drug-addicted—bad enough to believe in the stories that Charlie would tell them, including that he was the second coming of Jesus Christ, and that they had all been selected by Charlie to get ready for the upcoming Black uprising against the Whites.

On August 9th and 10th, 1969, Charlie ordered some of his Family to murder seven people in horrific ways before he was arrested. The Charlie Manson trial, which would be labeled as "The Helter Skelter Murders," would become the largest trial to date and was covered by all media throughout the world.

HOM: How did you come to write the Manson story?

GUINN: When I write nonfiction books, I usually pick an era in American history that interests me enough to write about. Once I have decided on the period, I then choose a significant event or a famous person. It's looking for the different threads that come together to make the moment possible for something to happen, such as the Sharon Tate and LaBianca murders.

HOM: So, Manson was just one of many doing what he was doing in the sixties. But did it turn out the way that he wanted it to?

GUINN: Yes. Charlie used the events of the counter-culture during the '60s to help attract his followers, yet he was very different himself.

HOM: So, in essence, Manson was just using these lifestyle trends of the time to get what he wanted for himself?

GUINN: Manson had been doing the same things that he did in the '60s back in both the '40s and '50s. He would take the best aspects of the counter-culture and adapt them to his own devices. While he was in prison in the 1950s, he developed a technique that he would later use in San

Francisco to attract people, as described in the book *How to Win Friends and Influence People*, written by Dale Carnegie.

HOM: That was an already popular book. Without Manson knowing it, he could attract others like himself who were not well-read. His followers would think that Manson himself created these ideas.

GUINN: Yes, Dale Carnegie permeated almost every part of the American culture back then. Somehow, Charlie, an uneducated guy from West Virginia, was able to use it horrifically.

HOM: How did he do that?

GUINN: When I interviewed both Patricia Krenwinkel and Leslie Van Houten while they were both still in Corona Women's Prison, I asked them both what it was that Charles Manson said to them that attracted them to him. They both answered, telling me several things that Charlie had told them, and everything he said to them was word for word from the Dale Carnegie book.

HOM: Do you remember any of it now?

GUINN: In Chapter 7, the idea was always to

make the other person think that the idea was theirs. Leslie Van Houten said that when she first met Charlie, he would compliment her on how smart she was and how well she understood the Bible. Manson would come up with the lyrics for his songs out of the blue, so after he learned that Leslie knew shorthand, he gave her the job of following him around while she carried a notebook with her so that she could write down his lyrics as he said them.

Another thing that Manson used from the Carnegie book was how most people were driven by their sex drive and the need to be famous. So he would lure men into his Family by promising as much sex as they wanted. And they would not only become famous but rule the world with him one day soon, after the race war that he called "Helter-Skelter" was over.

Manson utilized ideas that originated in the 1940s and were popularized by people in the 1960s, demonstrating that even though he wasn't an educated man, he was still a savvy one. Additionally, he was a skilled manipulator.

HOM: Do we know what Manson wanted to do with his life back when he was young? What did he want to become?

GUINN: It was strange. When Manson was first sent to prison for the car thefts he was convicted of, he found himself living amongst several pimps, who were also in jail for various reasons. Manson was able to learn how they were able to control their women and make them perform sex on other men for money to give him.

The most common practices were for the pimps to isolate the women from their families and close friends. While they would keep their women feeling needed, the pimps would also beat them, but only enough to keep them scared. Charlie would also learn how to identify the women's weaknesses or needs, only to use them later when he needed to.

HOM: Manson was also good at finding women and girls who were vulnerable, didn't he?

GUINN: Yes. Charlie also knew precisely where to go to find them. When he was released from prison, Charlie didn't head home. Instead, he went to the Haight-

Ashbury district in San Francisco. He knew that he couldn't get away with his plans in most towns found in the heartland. Charlie also knew that hundreds of teenagers were making their way to San Francisco every day, seeking something.

HOM: Now, Manson was released in '67, correct?

GUINN: Yes. The kids heading to Haight-Ashbury didn't know what they were looking for or what to expect. They all believed that this was the place to go for peace and love. Many of them were seeking a spiritual leader or guru to teach them how to live a happy life. This became the perfect place for Manson to find his victims.

HOM: Apparently, Manson would ask the girls he met and talked to to perform sex acts on him?

GUINN: Manson believed that it was the women's job to perform any sex act that the men wanted them to. And if they didn't, then they were not deserving of his attention. He would often arrange group sex get-togethers where he would choose who would have sex with whom and what they would do. He wanted to ensure that every woman had every man so that they moved around a lot, thereby preventing emotional attachments from forming.

HOM: Can you tell us how Scientology became involved and how Manson used it?

GUINN: It was the timing, as when Manson was placed in prison, the philosophy behind the American penal system had changed. It was no longer about retribution, where they would make the prisoners suffer. Instead, it became about reforming prisoners. The new focus introduced various programs and courses for inmates, designed to equip them with the necessary social skills to reintegrate into society.

So, it became normal for various religious groups, like Scientology, to be allowed in prisons as it gave prisoners support. The religion itself wasn't necessary. It was simply the fact that these religious organizations were adept at attracting people to join them. Far too many prisoners didn't have a lot of support from their families, and the religious group would accept them and often tell them how perfect they were and how much they were loved. Manson would also borrow stories from Scientology and adapt them to fit his narrative, modifying them as needed.

HOM: Now, I believe that Manson was heavily influenced by his devout Christian grandmother.

GUINN: I was able to locate Manson's sister and cousin while writing this book. Neither of them had ever been interviewed about Manson before. I was able to see several letters and photos of the Family, and I even obtained Manson's grandmother, Nancy Maddox's, study guide for the Bible. In this guide, she would make Charlie read over all the time to teach him good Christian values, which she had underlined in the book so that he would pay attention to specific passages.

Manson's grandmother belonged to a very fundamentalist church in McMechan, West Virginia, which she made him attend with her. That was part of the arrangement she made with the authorities to get him out of the reform school. She also required him to join a youth group for the church. It was in that youth group that he first heard about the "Book of Revelation," which discusses the end times.

However, Charlie was storing knowledge for

later use. When he discussed Helter Skelter and the apocalypse predicted for 1969 and got his followers to do some pretty warped things because of that prediction, he was pulling a lot of it right out of the "Book of Revelation."

HOM: When we get to the *White Album* by the Beatles, this played another vital role for Manson as he believed there were hidden messages in the words of the songs on that album.

GUINN: Manson used the Beatles' *White Album* just as he used the "Book of Revelations" as tools to brainwash his Family of followers. He would control what they listened to or watched, so the majority of it was the Beatles or his songs. By mid-1968, during their group gatherings, the *White Album* was played several times each night. Manson would often explain the meaning of each song when it played. Manson would play some songs repeatedly as he thought they were the key songs to convince his Family of what he wanted them to believe.

"Helter-Skelter" was an essential song for Manson to play as he said it was the imminent race war and the Beatles' message for him. It discussed how the Black community had been held down for too long. "Blackbird" represented the Black uprising against white supremacy. This thought always kept Manson on edge because during his very first days in prison, after Black Muslims roughed him up, he became terrified of all Black people. Then, after he was out, he ran into who he thought was a Black Panther in a drug deal gone bad and ended up shooting him. Manson equated his run-ins with Blacks to what the future held for America.

Manson believed and told his followers that there was going to be an apocalyptic race war very shortly, and they would all have to go to Death Valley to find what he called "The Bottomless Pit," where they would live until the war was over. According to the Bible, what came next was that the Blacks would win the race war but be intellectually inferior to the whites. Therefore, it was Manson's and the Family's job to come out of the bottomless pit and rule them as they were unable to do it themselves.

As almost all of his followers believed every word he told them without question, it demonstrated their devotion to Charlie. No matter what he told them, they thought it to be true, so when he told them that their only choices were to either come with him and be safe or leave to fight the Blacks to the death during the race war, they believed him.

HOM: Now, I believe that when you spoke with Leslie and Patricia, they believed in the upcoming race war or "Helter-Skelter?"

GUINN: Well, by then, anything Manson told them, they believed in without question. You also have to realize that, with all the women in his Family, they had a certain amount of fear of him. He often tested them and their loyalties, not only by making them have sex with him and the other men, but by other more threatening things. Manson would tell one of the women to go over and stand in front of a tree. After they did that, he would throw knives at them, hitting the tree above their heads. The more any of the women moved around or jumped when he threw a knife, the less that person trusted him. When he did this with Patricia, Manson hit her near her head and pinned her hair to the tree. He walked over and yanked the knife out of the tree, which pulled her hair from her scalp. This made Patricia scared of Charlie, and she always worried that he would hurt her.

When I spoke to Leslie, her mind was on how great life was going to be in the "bottomless pit" because Charlie promised there would be lots of drugs there for everyone. Another thing that excited her was that Charlie had told them they would be able to change their bodies in any way they wanted during their time in the bottomless pit. Leslie had fantasies of becoming an elf and growing wings. Later, after her arrest, she worried that her wings would grow on her back while she was in prison, which shows how deeply she truly believed in Charlie.

HOM: What did you learn from Leslie and Patricia about the Family's LSD get-togethers every night?

GUINN: Not only did I hear about them from those two, but several other people who got involved in these get-togethers. Manson would always give each participant the LSD, often placing it in their mouth himself. He also would take LSD himself, only a much lighter dose than he gave to the others.

After everyone began to get high on the LSD, Manson would start some performances. He might grab his guitar and sing some of his songs, or he might stage a show where he played Jesus Christ and reenacted the crucifixion in front of his followers, which would support their belief in him as the second coming.

Most of the shows went smoothly, and everyone easily got into whatever Charlie was doing. But there were a few times when one of his Family members would get fidgety or begin to make noises or talk because of their reaction to the drugs. Manson would get angry because they were taking the attention away from his performance. Sometimes, he became so mad that he would begin to hit whoever was making the noise with a chair or whatever was handy, and he would continue to hit them until they lay quietly on the ground. After that, he could continue his performance.

HOM: Did you find out how his followers were preparing for Helter-Skelter in Death Valley?

GUINN: Manson first needed to get as many vehicles as he could, so he began having his followers go out and steal as many cars or dune buggies as they could. He also needed any of the stolen vehicles that weren't dune buggies to be converted into them so that they could travel through the desert.

Manson was then trying to recruit some of the bikers from the Straight Satans or any other biker gang he could find. Those new members could not only work on cars but also act as protectors, as they all knew how to fight. Manson's paranoia was getting stronger, so he was having holders for weapons welded to the dune buggies so that they could all be carried if the Black Panthers began their attack. He also started to put people on patrol all day and night who had guns and were ready in case of an attack.

During the daytime, he would have small teams. Usually, men went out into the desert to search for the bottomless pit, while he had the women searching for food, which was typically some plant. There wasn't much available, and often, they would almost starve to death.

Manson would have to travel to Los Angeles, attempt to obtain money from acquaintances, such as Dennis Wilson, and then purchase food before returning to Barker Ranch. Patricia recounted times when they would have to live off a small bag of rice, powdered milk, and cinnamon. Most of them were far too tired and weak to put up very much resistance to Manson's wishes.

HOM: Let's talk about how Manson got to know Dennis Wilson.

GUINN: For Charlie, it started when he was forced to go to his grandmother's church. He would have to sing in the choir, and he had a good voice. During that time, he was particularly fond of Frankie Laine's music.

HOM: When did Manson first hear the Beatles?

GUINN: It was when Charlie was in prison in 1964 or 1965, while he was in the workshop, and he could listen to the radio. At that time, it seemed like every second song was by a band named the Beatles. Charlie not only liked their music, but he was impressed by how everyone was now talking about them. This is what inspired Charlie to pick up a guitar and begin writing his songs, as he aspired to achieve the fame of the Beatles.

After Charlie was released from prison, he developed a desire to become famous, just like the Beatles. So, he needed to get somebody who was powerful in the record business to help him make it.

Once he moved to Los Angeles, he began sending his girls out to look for rock stars. Remember, this was also the time when there were lots of drugs and free sex going on, and so having the girls out there, it wouldn't be long before he would find a few. One day, while Dennis Wilson, the drummer of the Beach Boys, was driving on Sunset Boulevard, he saw two women hitchhiking on the side of the road. He stopped and invited them to take them back to his house for some milk and cookies. They had no idea that Wilson was a famous rock star or who the Beach Boys were, as they never listened to that kind of music.

When the girls returned to Spahn Ranch, Charlie wanted to know if they had met anybody important. They told Charlie about a guy named Dennis, who was a drummer from a band they had never heard of before, the Beach Boys.

Manson got excited with the news and packed up the girls and several Family members, having them take everyone back to Wilson's house. Later that night, when Wilson returned home, he found Manson and his Family members inside, playing a Beatles album on the record player. Most of Charlie's girls were naked, and everyone was using drugs. It wasn't long before Wilson got comfortable and joined in.

Manson and his Family soon moved in, and during their stay, Manson played his songs for Wilson to listen to. Denis liked them, so he decided to set up a demo for Charlie with the Beach Boys' record label, thinking maybe they would record him. When his brothers heard Manson, they felt that he was a talentless bum, and it never went anywhere.

Neil Young heard Charlie next and loved that he was able to improvise. And he asked his label to give him a chance, but they weren't interested either. John Phillips, who was in the Mamas and the Papas, also wasn't interested when he heard Charlie. An agent, Rudi Altobelli, for several other singers, including Buffy Sainte-Marie, didn't like Manson and said that he had nothing special to offer.

Even after all that rejection, Charlie still believed he could secure a record contract. He had now set his sights on Terry Melcher, a record producer and the son of Doris Day. Melcher had been successfully producing hits for the Los Angeles rock and roll scene.

HOM: I think he was producing The Byrds then?

GUINN: Yes, The Byrds, but he was also known for taking small garage bands and making them into stars. He did that with a band he called Paul Revere and the Raiders, which he had outfitted in Revolutionary War costumes. Over the course of just three years, he had successfully produced around 80 hit singles.

If Terry Melcher thought Manson had any talent, he would have signed him to a record deal with Columbia Records. When Melcher heard Manson during his audition on Spahn Ranch after he told Manson that he had no idea what he would do with him, he left and told others that he thought Manson was nothing more than one of 100 other long-haired types trying to be the Beatles. However, Manson had no real sales ability.

After being rejected by Melcher, he felt like he had failed in front of his Family. He needed to come up with something new that would keep his followers with him. This is what became one major part, not the only reason, but the driving reason for the Sharon Tate and LaBianca murders.

HOM: What was Charlie trying to say in his song "Cease to Exist?" I ask that because that was the song that Dennis Wilson took, changed, and then recorded for one of the Beach Boys' albums. It sounds to me like what he was saying was that girls should give up their world, be with him, and cease to exist, and their submission is a gift?

GUINN: Yes. That's what I think made Manson angry—not only claiming the song as his own, written by Dennis, but also changing the lyrics of the song. Manson had told Wilson on several occasions that he could change the music but never the lyrics. It would change the whole meaning that Charlie wanted the young women to know when they listened to the song.

HOM: Wilson did leave the line "cease to exist" in the Beach Boys' version, didn't he? But I guess changed the title of the song to "Never Learn Not to Love?"

GUINN: Yes. Only Wilson changed the meaning of the song, removing the fact that it was addressed to a girl, which angered Manson.

HOM: So, you're saying that because Manson couldn't achieve his dream of getting a record contract and becoming a rock star, for him to keep his followers, he had to do something else, and that was murder?

GUINN: The followers of any leader or guru begin to leave when they see that leader lose at something. He was already seeing some of his long-term followers run away from him. Now, he needed to do something that would recapture their attention. Along came the racial tension that turned into riots in major cities, including Watts. This gave him something to work with.

It was just then that he had a drug deal that went bad, and Manson ended up shooting a man whom he thought was a member of the Black Panther Party. This made Charlie believe that the Panthers would retaliate and attack him at Spahn Ranch.

Then Manson and the Family felt that Gary Hinman ripped them off on a drug deal. So Bobby Beausoleil, who was a friend of Charlie's, took two of Manson's women and went to Hinman's house to get the money back. After torturing Hinman for a while, he still wouldn't give them any money, so Beausoleil called Manson.

Charlie comes to Hinman's house in the middle of the night, cuts off part of his ear with his sword, and leaves, telling Beausoleil, "You know what to do." This meant for him to kill Hinman and make it look like it was a murder that the Black Panthers committed.

Afterward, when Beausoleil is driving Hinman's car that he stole after the murder, police arrest him. In the car, he is carrying the knife that killed Hinman, and also has his blood on it. Manson became worried that Beausoleil would inform the police about what had happened.

Manson then began to coax the Family into thinking that they needed to create a copycat murder, also with signs that the Black Panthers did it, while Bobby was still in jail. This would lead the cops to believe that he couldn't have done it, and they would have to let him go. Manson also thought that it would be best to murder celebrities or rich people to get the attention that he wanted. He also tells his Family that if they could make it look like Black militants did it, this would start Helter-Skelter. The Whites would be angry, and the Blacks would fight back. Meanwhile, they'll be in the desert.

Now, they would have to select the right place to do it. They chose the house that Melcher had lived in on Cielo Drive. Manson knew that Melcher didn't live there anymore, but whoever was living there now must be rich and famous.

Manson sent out Tex Watson, Linda Kasabian, Susan Atkins, and Patricia Krenwinkel that night. Watson had been to the house before, so he knew how to get there. They chose that house not because Melcher lived there but because they knew Sharon Tate now lived there, and they knew how to get to the house. It was the location that decided the fate of those five people that night.

HOM: Who was with Sharon Tate that night?

GUINN: We had gained new information about that night of the murder from Patricia Krenwinkel. She had never told her complete story before, but finally did for me. Patricia would walk me through the whole night, hour by hour. It was pretty horrifying.

HOM: What did she tell you that was the most horrifying?

GUINN: Probably the part when she was chasing Abigail Folger out onto the back lawn of the house and stabbing her over and over again. She would describe how her knife was hitting the bone so hard that it hurt her hand. Instead, she would stab Abigail where her organs were so that it was more comfortable.

HOM: Manson wanted the murders to be something spectacular so that it would grab the attention of the press, correct?

GUINN: Yes. Not only did Manson plan out these murders ahead of time, but he returned to the crime scene later that same night to make sure that everything was left correctly. He got into a car and took the killers back with him to Cielo Drive. When they arrived and walked into the house, Manson noticed a large American flag. So he took it and draped it over the sofa right beside where Sharon Tate's murdered body lay. He wanted it to be very visual and might trigger a race riot. Charlie then could tell his followers he was right.

HOM: What did Manson do to try to connect the murders to the Black Panthers?

GUINN: Well, he tried to leave signs for the cops that it was the Black Panthers. Like at the Hinman house, he had them leave what looked like a pawprint on the wall using the victim's blood as well as the word "pig," which was a slang word for police. That word wasn't only used by the Panthers. It was also used by all the young white protesters of the day. But this is why they left the word "pig" on the Polanski front door at Cielo Drive.

They did all of this thinking that the cops would think that the Black Panthers did the murders. But that never happened. This would make Manson angry when he woke up the next day, on the tenth, and he decided that they needed to do the same thing over again the following night. Only this time, he would be with them to ensure everything was done correctly.

HOM: This is what led to the Leno and Rosemary LaBianca murders?

GUINN: Yes. This time, Manson picked the house where many of them had partied before, only it was now vacant. Manson noticed the next-door house, and it became the misfortune of the LaBiancas to have been home that night.

HOM: Have you heard from anybody from the Manson Family?

GUINN: Manson had very kindly left my contact information with his current followers, and I have heard from a few of them. They are an interesting group of people, and I didn't think that they would be. Some of them are brilliant people who I believe have just chosen the wrong person to admire.

HOM: Has anybody threatened you because you wrote about Manson?

GUINN: I have had a few threats, but they are from the kind of people who use crayons to write, so there is nothing to be concerned about.

HOM: Do you know how many followers Manson has now?

GUINN: Somewhere in the hundreds and spread out all through the country.

HOM: Are they actual followers or just fans?

GUINN: I don't think that Manson differentiates between the two because he likes to stay in touch with anybody who is devoted to him. Many of them want him to be released so that he can lead them in life.

HOM: But why would people follow him now that we know he was behind several murders?

GUINN: Some people just believe in things because it's what they want and not the facts, so Manson saying that he didn't kill anyone is all that they need to hear.

HOM: What happened when you approached Manson for an interview?

GUINN: It was a long time before he wrote back to me, and it wasn't a charming letter. I think he knew that I had been talking to people who had never spoken out before, and he knew that if I wrote a book, it would expose all the lies he had told over the years. So, the letter was negative. However, when the book was nearing completion, I asked for permission to use some of his artwork in it, and he agreed. However, I think that since then, he has become famous, albeit for being notorious.

PART III
THE VICTIMS

Bernard "Lotsapoppa" Crowe

Bernie Crowe, otherwise known as "Lotsapoppa," was a Los Angeles drug dealer who got mixed up with the Manson Family to conduct a drug deal. In the early Summer of 1969, when Charlie was doing almost anything to try and get the money together so the Family could move out to Death Valley, Tex Watson came up with a plan to make some money. He approached his ex-girlfriend, Luella, who sold small amounts of marijuana around town. When he called her, he said, "Hey, the Family has one hundred dollars and wanted to buy a kilo of grass, but our mafia vending-machine connection would only sell us 25 kilos at a throw, for a cool $2,500."

Tex didn't have any mafia connection who was going to sell him 25 kilos of pot, what he wanted was for her to give him the $2,500, and he would disappear without giving her any drugs.

An hour later, Luella called Tex back and told her that she had found someone interested in buying the extra kilos that the Family didn't want, but she also wanted to make some money from the deal. He agreed to give her 3 kilos of the pot, and she arranged to have Tex meet her guy, Bernie Crowe/Lotsapoppa.

They would all meet at Luella's place, but once Crowe saw Tex, he told them that he would have to accompany them to make the drug deal. Crowe led Tex and Luella out to his car, where he had two of his bodyguards waiting for him. They all got in the car and left.

Tex gave Crowe, who was driving, directions to an apartment building, and they parked the car. Before Crowe handed Tex the cash, he told him that they were keeping his girl as collateral until he got back. Tex took the money and got out of the car, telling them he would be right back. Tex disappeared into the front door of the building, and while Crowe, Luella, and the two bodyguards waited in the car, Tex snuck out of the side of the building and headed for Spahn Ranch.

By the time Tex returned to the ranch with the cash, Charlie had already gotten a call from Crowe asking where he was. Charlie told Crowe that Tex hadn't been around for a couple of weeks, and he didn't know where he was. Crowe became angry and told Charlie that he wanted his cash back, or he and his crew would visit the ranch, and nobody would be left alive.

Charlie grabbed a gun and Family member T.J. (Thomas Wallerman), as he knew where this Crowe guy lived. They left the ranch. Manson planned to have the gun placed in his pants on his backside. He would be walking in front of T.J., and once they entered Crowe's place, T.J. was to pull the gun out and shoot Crowe.

When they entered Crowe's apartment, two other people were standing in the main room beside Crowe. T.J. panicked, turned around, and ran out the front door. Manson grabbed the gun and shot Crowe in his chest, and he fell to the ground. The other two men started to run towards Manson, but he pointed his gun at them and told them to stop. Manson slowly backed out of the apartment and caught up to T.J., and they drove off.

On the drive back to the ranch, Manson told T.J. how angry he was with him for backing out of the kill and running away. He threatened him several times, and once they returned to the ranch, T.J. grabbed the items he had stored there and took off.

Manson quietly returned to his place, saying nothing.

The next day, when Manson got up, he saw on the news that a member of the Black Panther Party had been shot and killed the night before. Manson began bragging to the Family, telling them all that he had murdered the panther. Only now would they all have to be prepared for the panthers to strike back at them at any time.

In reality, Crowe was not only not a Black Panther, but he wasn't dead. He would soon recover from his gunshot wound and would be called in as a witness for the Manson trial, which completely shocked Manson as he thought Crowe was dead.

Gary Hinman

"You can't judge me, and there is no possible
way to feel any remorse. Only God can judge
me, and God is on my side."

Gary Hinman was found dead at his home at 964
Old Topanga Canyon Road on July 31, 1969. He had
been stabbed twice in his heart and had several cuts
across the left side of his face. Hinman's home had
been ransacked, and his blood had been used to
write "Political Piggy" on his living room wall. Both
of Hinman's cars were also gone. Police marked
this as a cold case and believed that it had been just
another of the strange hippie weirdo crimes that
were prevalent at the time in Los Angeles.

Hinman was born in Colorado on December 24, 1934, and was working on obtaining his doctorate in Sociology at the University of California, Los Angeles (UCLA). However, he was known as a peaceful man who was a Zen Buddhist, musician, and piano teacher.

Hinman also had a home-made mescaline factory in his basement, which was primarily for his use. However, he was also known to have sold it to his friends and classmates.

Less than a week after the murder, Bobby Beausoleil was found sleeping in the back of Hinman's Fiat Station Wagon by a highway patrol officer near San Luis Obispo. Beausoleil claimed that the car broke down while he was en route to San Francisco. Police were also suspicious as Beausoleil didn't have a driver's license and was carrying a knife with him. They arrested him and later charged him with the murder of Hinman.

It was three days later that the murders at the Polanski-Tate household took place. Initially, the police didn't connect the Hinman murder with the Tate murders, which surprised Beausoleil. He thought that with "Political Pig" written on Hinman's wall and "Pig" written on Tate's wall, the police would connect the murders and let him go.

Beausoleil was first brought to trial for Hinman's murder in November 1969, but it ended in a hung jury. The second trial took place the following Spring in March 1970, only this time, the prosecution upped it to a death penalty case. Detectives got Danny DeCarlo to turn state's evidence against Beausoleil in exchange for complete immunity on a dozen charges against him, which included everything from drug dealing, car theft, and gun smuggling. Beausoleil was convicted of Hinman's murder and received the death penalty. Two years later, California repealed the death penalty, and therefore, Beausoleil's sentence was reduced to life in prison.

Beausoleil claimed to be innocent for the next ten years. During the Summer of 1980, he confessed to Ann Louise Bardach during an interview with her at Tracy Prison. On the night before Hinman was murdered, Beausoleil was at the Spahn Ranch, where he was spending the night with Charles Manson. He was not only there to visit with Manson, but he was also making a delivery of one thousand mescaline pills to the club treasurer of the Straight Satan's motorbike gang, Danny DeCarlo. The delivery ultimately became an issue, as the bikers soon realized that the mescaline was not real and became angry, demanding that their money be returned to them.

On the following morning, when Beausoleil got up, he was going to go back to Hinman's house and not only demand his money be returned but also confront Hinman about selling fake drugs through him. When two of Manson's girls, Susan (Sadie) Atkins and Mary Bruner, heard that Beausoleil was going to Hinman's house, they asked to go along, as they liked Hinman.

Beausoleil claimed that he only went to Hinman's house to get the thousand dollars he had given Hinman the day before to pay for the drugs that Danny DeCarlo wanted. He also claimed that he wouldn't have brought Adkins and Bruner with him if his intention was murder. Bruner had been with Hinman before and even stayed with him a few times.

After they arrived at Hinman's house, Beausoleil demanded the thousand dollars back from him so he could take it back to the Satan motorcycle gang, but Hinman refused. Beausoleil then began searching the house for something worth a thousand dollars so that he could take it back to the gang instead.

Beausoleil gave Susan Atkins his gun and told her to watch Hinman, and he told her to shoot Hinman if he moved from the kitchen table. Once Beausoleil was out of the kitchen and scouting around for something valuable, Hinman jumped to try to get the gun from Atkins, who then began to scream for help. By the time Beausoleil got back into the kitchen, Hinman had the weapon. Then the two of them began to wrestle for it. The gun went off, but it never hit Hinman. Instead, it went through the kitchen sink. That's when Beausoleil grabbed his knife from his belt, and the two men struggled to fight. Eventually, Hinman agreed to sign the title of both his cars over to Beausoleil to pay the $1,000 owed.

After the fight ended, Beausoleil even sewed up Hinman's cut ear with some dental floss from his bathroom, and everything was calm for a while. According to Beausoleil, Hinman only died after that because he had threatened to go to the police and charge him with assault. Beausoleil was surprised, as he had figured that everything had been settled after he turned over the two vehicles to him. Neither car combined would be worth a thousand dollars, but they would hopefully be enough for the biker gang.

Beausoleil then called Bruce Davis at the Spahn Ranch and asked him to come over and get one of the cars. David arrived and only went into the house to retrieve the car keys. Then he left. He was not involved in the murder, but the prosecutor later charged and convicted him of being part of the

Hinman murder. Hinman wasn't murdered until long after David had picked up his car.

It was when Hinman threatened Beausoleil that he was going to the police and he would be charged with assault that Beausoleil decided to kill him. He felt that Hinman was more respected in the city as he owned his own home and was a college student. So he stabbed Hinman in the heart twice, and he died instantly.

Susan Atkins seemed to enjoy the fighting and even the murder of Hinman. So much so that she placed a pillow over his face, thinking that it would do something to him. He was already dead. Bruner, on the other hand, was scared and more upset, as she was much closer to Hinman than the others were. Atkins was the one who wrote on the wall with Hinman's blood, but it was Beausoleil's idea to hopefully take the police off their trail. He also figured that because Hinman was a known hippie communist, he could make it look like the murderer might be one of Hinman's cohorts.

When they returned to Spahn Ranch, Beausoleil returned the gun to Davis and never told him or anybody what had happened there. But later, Atkins, called "motor-mouth" by Beausoleil, told Danny DeCarlo. After he was arrested, the story reached the district attorney, which allowed

DeCarlo to turn state's evidence to avoid the charges against him for testifying against Beausoleil.

During Beausoleil's trial, it was said that Manson came to the house when Hinman was still alive and sliced off one of his ears with a knife. It was said that he ordered them to kill Hinman. But Beausoleil disagreed with that. He said that it was said only because the Sheriff wanted to involve Charles in the murder. He also claimed that Hinman's ear wasn't sliced off. It had only been cut when he sliced Hinman's face.

When Beausoleil was asked if he thought the Manson Family did the Tate and LaBianca murders and had the blood of their victims being used to write messages on the walls of their homes to try and help get him released, he somewhat agreed with that.

"I do believe there was something to that, yes, because of the way the murders were made to look. The murders were a few days after I was arrested. I don't think that whoever's idea it was to commit these murders would have been able to get the participation of those involved unless there had been this noble concept."

Sharon Tate

On January 24, 1943, Sharon Tate was born in Dallas, Texas, to Colonel Paul Tate, an intelligence officer in the U.S. Army, and his wife, Doris. She was the eldest of three daughters born to the couple.

Sharon found herself at the center of attention from the early age of six months, after being given the title of "Miss Tiny Tot of Dallas" for winning a beauty contest. Throughout her school years, her father was transferred frequently, and the whole family had to relocate with him. By the time Sharon graduated from American High School in Vicenza, Italy, in June 1961, it would have been her sixth school and sixth city she had attended.

Before graduating, despite having moved several times to different cities, she often entered beauty contests and won. In 1959, Sharon won the "Miss Richland" contest when she was sixteen. She was eligible for the "Miss Washington" contest because of that win, but her father was transferred to Verona, Italy, before she could enter.

While in Verona, Italy, Sharon and some of her friends were watching the movie *Hemingway's Adventure of a Young Man* being filmed. Actor Richard Beymer spotted her in the crowd, and the two began to date. During that time, Beymer would talk her into being an extra on the film. Afterward, Sharon appeared in one of the episodes of *The Pat Boone Chevy Showroom*, which was also being filmed in Venice, Italy.

Later in 1959, Sharon would become an extra in the movie *Barabbas*, as it was also being filmed in Verona, Italy. The star of the movie, Jack Palance, was impressed with Tate and arranged for her to take a screen test in Rome.

In 1962, the Tate family returned to the United States and settled in Los Angeles. Once there, Sharon got in touch with Richard Beymer's agent, Harold Gefsky, whom Beymer had introduced her to earlier. Gefsky signed Sharon up as one of his clients and began securing her work in commercials on television and in magazines.

Only one year later, Tate got a seven-year contract with Filmways, where she began getting small parts in television shows such as *Mister Ed* and *The Beverly Hillbillies*. Also in 1963, Tate met the French actor Philippe Forquet, and they had a whirlwind relationship. In less than a year, they went from dating to becoming engaged, only to break up.

After their breakup in 1964, she met Jay Sebring at a party, and they began dating. Sebring was a well-known hairstylist to several film stars at the time. He was married at the time, but that relationship wasn't going well and would end in divorce by early 1965. Within a year of the pair dating, Sebring asked Tate to marry him. But she said no as she didn't want to get married until she was ready to retire from acting.

Tate then went to London to film a low-budget film. There, she met Roman Polanski at a nightclub. Later, he cast her in a movie he was making in Italy, *The Fearless Vampire Killer*, provided she would wear a red-haired wig. During the filming, the two began to date, and by the time the production was completed, Tate had moved in with Polanski at his London apartment.

Sebring traveled to London to see Tate and was devastated when he found out that she was in a new relationship with Polanski, but the two men met and soon became good friends.

Tate returned to America to make a film, *Don't Make Waves*, with star Tony Curtis. Polanski soon followed her back to the United States to begin filming *Rosemary's Baby*. The couple moved in together and continued their relationship.

Tate then landed her most prominent film role to date, *Valley of the Dolls*, which was released in late 1967 and received generally negative reviews. Despite poor reviews, she was nominated for a Golden Globe award for her performance in the film.

The couple were married on January 20, 1968, in London, UK, and they moved into his home at Eaton Square in London. In the latter part of 1968, the couple moved to the Chateau Marmot in Los Angeles, where they remained until they were able to rent Patty Duke's home in Beverly Hills. While they were living there, the couple often hosted parties where the house would be filled with strangers. Leslie Caron said that they were trusting to the point of being reckless.

The couple struggled as Polanski wanted them to remain open sexually, but Tate didn't like that.

However, she had accepted this when they got married. Tate was once quoted as saying, "We have a good arrangement. Roman lies to me, and I pretend to believe him."

During the summer of '68, Tate began working on one of the Dean Martin "Matt Helm" comedy detective films, *The Wrecking Crew*. This film would ultimately earn Tate her first set of positive reviews for her performance. Tate was now able to demand a $150,000 fee to act in her next film.

At the end of the year, Tate became pregnant. The couple moved to the home on Cielo Drive in Benedict Canyon in February 1969, which had previously been rented by Terry Melcher and his girlfriend, Candice Bergen. They had known the house very well, as they were friends with Melcher and had attended several of his parties.

Only a month later, in March, she flew to Italy to begin filming in the Orson Welles project *The Thirteen Chairs*. During the same time, Polanski went to London to make *The Day of the Dolphin*. Tate had finished her work first and returned home on July 20, 1969, where she had friends Abigail Folger and Wojciech Frykowski move in to look after their place while they were gone.

Once she returned, she asked them to stay on as Roman would be away for a while longer, finishing his project. Polanski was set to be home on August 12th, which was before the due date for the birth of their baby.

On August 8th, Roman called Sharon from London to tell her that he would be arriving home later than expected. Later that same night, around 8 p.m., Sharon, along with Sebring, Frykowski, and Folger, decided to go out to the Mexican restaurant El Coyote for dinner. All of them got back to Tate's Cielo Drive home somewhere around 10:30 p.m.

During their dinner, Folger and Frykowski were having a disagreement and bickered with each other. By the time they arrived home, they were no longer speaking to each other. Folger went directly to her bedroom, where she got ready for bed, grabbed a book, and began reading. Frykowski grabbed a blanket and went to the sofa, where he fell asleep.

Meanwhile, both Sharon and Sebring went to her room so that they could avoid the drama of Folger and Frykowski's fighting with each other. They both became comfortable and began discussing various Hollywood stars and the gossip they had heard.

In about two hours from then, all four would be murdered, along with Steve Parent, who happened to be visiting the property caretaker in the guest house located on the back of the property. Later, Charles Manson, along with Tex Watson, Susan Atkins, and Patricia Krenwinkel, were all convicted of the five murders.

Jay Sebring

Jay Sebring moved to Los Angeles after serving four years in the Navy during the Korean War. He was born Thomas John Kummer on October 10, 1933, in the state of Alabama. After moving to Los Angeles, he decided to change his name to suit his new business, which focused on creating modern men's hairstyles and cuts. His new name and brand would become Jay Sebring. Jay was taken from the first letter of his middle name, and Sebring was named after a Florida raceway.

It wasn't long before he had become popular among the male celebrities of the time. He was styling hair for Steve McQueen, Warren Beatty, and Kirk Douglas, who later asked him to do all the hair for the cast of the movie *Spartacus*.

Sebring was now making enough money to buy the former home of Jean Harlow in Benedict Canyon. One of the reasons Sebring liked the house was its haunting history, given that many people had died there. Harlow's husband, Paul Bern, hanged himself in one of the bathrooms in the house just three months after moving in. Later, one of the maids also died at the house. A total of four more people would end up committing suicide there, along with a guest who ended up drowning in the pool one night.

Even though Sebring had just married model Cami in early 1964, they divorced less than a year later, in March 1965. When he met Sharon Tate at one of the Hollywood parties, Sharon and Jay became a couple. Soon after, he asked Sharon to marry him. She said that she needed time to think about it and left for London, England, to appear in the Roman Polanski film called *The Fearless Vampire Killers*. It was during that filming that Tate and Polanski began dating and fell in love. Tate ended her relationship with Sebring via a phone call while she was still in London.

In 1968, when Tate and Polanski got married, it was reported that Jay attended the wedding and had become a close friend of Roman over the last couple of years. By the Summer of 1969, Sebring owned and operated four hair salons: the original one in West Hollywood, as well as locations in Palm Springs, Las Vegas, and the newest in San Francisco. He was also selling his own line of hair care products.

On August 8, 1969, Jay and Sharon went to dinner at the El Coyote restaurant with friends Abigail Folger and Wojciech Frykowski. After dinner, they returned to Tate's house on Cielo Drive. It was reported at the time of the murders that Jay and Sharon were in her bedroom, sitting on her bed, talking when three of the Manson Family, Charles, Tex Watson, Patricia Krenwinkel, and Susan Atkins, broke into the house and entered the bedroom. When they came into the bedroom, Sebring attempted to defend Tate and told the intruders that she was pregnant. Watson just shot him, and he fell to the floor. He kicked him several times in his face, which broke his nose, and then stabbed Sebring seven times.

Jim Markham, a friend of Sebring's in 2019, told *The Hollywood Reporter*, "I believe Manson had gone to the house to sell cocaine and marijuana the day before the murders. He met with Jay Sebring and Wojciech Frykowski at the gate on the driveway and looked over what Manson was selling. Instead of buying the drugs, they roughed Manson up at the gate. The next night, Manson sent some of the members of the Family up to the house to retaliate."

After the murders, police did find drugs in Sebring's Porsche, including marijuana, heroin, and some pills (mescaline or what was called speed back then). There were rumors about Sebring that he was not only using drugs but also selling them.

Abigail Folger

"Gibby," or Abigail Folger, was born on August 11, 1943, in San Francisco, to the Folger Coffee Chairman and President, Peter Folger, and socialite Inez Majia. Before she turned ten, her parents divorced. There were stories of extreme cruelty during her life, and her mother claimed that the reason was that when Abigail turned seventeen, her father remarried his thirty-four-year-old private secretary, Beverly.

Gibby remained focused on her arts, playing the piano, and hanging out with San Francisco's high society. In 1961, she made her official debut at the St. Francis Hotel and also graduated from Santa Catalina, a Catholic girls' school in Monterey,

California. In the Fall of 1961, she attended Radcliffe College in Cambridge, Massachusetts, where she starred in two plays with the Gilbert & Sullivan Players and later graduated with honors in 1964.

Abigail then attended Harvard, where she earned a degree in Art History in 1967. She later returned to California, where she took a full-time job as the Publicity Director of the Art Museum at the University of California, Berkeley. However, this job wouldn't last long. Neither would the next couple of jobs, which were both in New York. She didn't need to work, as she already had an annual income of $130,000 from Folgers Coffee. A year later, living in New York, she felt more freedom, as she wasn't as well-known there as she was in California.

While Abigail was working at a bookstore in New York in the early part of 1968, she met aspiring Polish writer Wojciech Frykowski at a party, and the two had an immediate connection. Within a month, he moved in with her at her New York apartment. As Frykowski was still relatively new in the country, he wasn't working. She ended up having to support the two of them.

In the Spring of 1968, the couple found themselves devoting much of their time and a significant portion of their money to working on Robert F.

Kennedy's presidential campaign. Abigail believed in everything Kennedy was doing and saying. In June of the same year, after Kennedy was assassinated in Los Angeles, she decided to rent a car, and the couple did a cross-country drive, ending up back in California.

Folger found a house in Laurel Canyon to rent, located at 2774 Woodstock Road, right across the street from where singer Cass Elliot lived. After the couple moved into the home, she bought a brand new yellow 1969 Firebird.

Wojciech quickly got in touch with Roman after they settled, and the four of them began to hang out regularly, going to parties and clubs together. Abigail and Frykowski soon met hairdresser Jay Sebring through Sharon, and he joined them regularly.

Abigail was dedicated to doing charity work and became a volunteer social worker for the Los Angeles County Welfare Department. She even attended fundraisers to help aid the Haight-Ashbury Free Medical Clinic in San Francisco during the same time when several of the Manson Family girls were there being treated for drug use.

On March 15, 1969, the day before Roman Polanski was to leave for London to begin working on his new movie, they had a party at their house on Cielo

Drive. There were well over one hundred attendees, including Jane and Peter Fonda, Tony Curtis, Warren Beatty, and the Mamas and the Papas. During that party, four uninvited men were causing trouble and fighting with the guests, so Roman asked them to leave.

About a week later, on March 23rd, Abigail and Wojciech went to have dinner with Sharon at her Cielo Drive home, as Tate was heading to Rome, Italy, the following day to start work on her latest film. Jay Sebring and a few other guests were also in attendance for the dinner.

While they were at the table in the dining room, which faced the front, they all noticed a strange-looking man on the front lawn, simply walking around and examining the surroundings. One of Sharon's friends and photographer, Shahrokh Hatami, got up and went out the front door, approaching the man. He asked the man what he wanted and what he was doing there. The stranger asked him if Terry Melcher was home, but Hatami didn't know who that was and told him that the house belonged to Roman and Sharon Polanski. The man left but was later identified as Charles Manson.

On April 1st, Abigail and Wojciech moved into Polanski's house. Roman wanted them to be there to look after the place while they were away. Abigail decided to take a break from volunteering for a while and focus on her relationship with Wojciech. By now, they had begun to fight regularly and were starting to use drugs daily.

Abigail got word that Sharon Tate had finished filming and would be returning home on July 20th, so she and Wojciech began to move some of their belongings back to their home on Woodstock Road.

When Tate returned home, she asked Folger and Wojciech if they would mind staying at the house with her until Roman returned from London, which was scheduled for August 12th. They agreed. That same night, after she returned home, they would all watch the moon landing on television.

On the evening of August 9, 1969, Tate, along with Jay Sebring, Abigail Folger, and Wojciech, all decided to go to El Coyote, a Mexican restaurant, for dinner. After they returned home, Tate retired to her bedroom with Sebring while Abigail went to her room by herself to read a book. Wojciech remained in the living room by himself. Abigail and Wojciech were not getting along very well that night and had an argument at dinner, so Wojciech decided to go to sleep on the couch.

At about ten that evening, the phone rang, and it was Abigail's mother calling to confirm their plans for the weekend. Abigail was flying out to San Francisco the following morning to celebrate her mother's birthday together.

Wojciech Frykowski

Wojciech Frykowski was born in Poland on December 22, 1936. Even though he received his degree in chemistry, he preferred to be with his writer and filmmaker friends. When he met Roman Polanski, Polanski was a doorman at a school dance. After Polanski refused to let Frykowski into the dance due to his reputation for trouble, the two of them got into a physical fight.

A few weeks after that incident, the two ran into each other again, this time at a local bar. Wojciech bought drinks and had them sent to Polanski's table. After that, the two began talking. Eventually, they became best friends.

When Polanski made his first movie, *Knife in the Water*, he hired Frykowski as a lifeguard for it.

During this time, Frykowski was married and divorced twice. The famous Polish author Agnieszka Osiecka was one of his wives. He had one son, Bartek.

Frykowski moved to New York in 1967, and it was there that he met Abigail Folger. The two of them hit it off immediately. Even though Frykowski didn't speak English and Folger didn't speak Polish, the two were fluent in French. The two moved into an apartment in New York, but by the Summer of 1968, they decided to move to the Hollywood Hills in California, where they rented a house across the street from singer Mama Cass.

In the Spring of 1969, the couple moved into Polanski's house while they were away making movies. Sharon returned home first from her last project, so Roman told the couple to stay at the house until he got back in August. So, they continued to live at the house even though they were not getting along very well and found themselves fighting regularly. Because of their arguing and Sharon being pregnant, Sharon no longer wanted them at the house and constantly complained to Roman and her friends. Frykowski was rumored to be not only using several drugs but, during one of the many parties he had at the house, had met some drug dealers and began dealing himself. More gossip has emerged that there might have been a connection between the drug dealers, Wojciech, and the Manson Family as well, but nothing concrete.

On August 8, 1969, Wojciech and Abigail were dining with Sharon Tate and Jay Sebring at the El Coyote Restaurant and then returned to the house with them. Once they returned, Wojciech went to sleep on the living room sofa while Abigail went to their bedroom, got into bed, and started reading a book. Sharon and Jay were in Sharon's bedroom and were gossiping about Hollywood stars.

Frykowski was woken up shortly after midnight by Charles Tex Watson. When he asked him what time it was, he proceeded to kick him in the head. Frykowski got up off the floor and asked him who he was. Tex said, "I'm the devil, and I'm here to do the devil's business."

While this was going on, the Manson girls searched the house, found everyone, and forced them out into the living room at knife point. Watson had told Susan Atkins to tie Frykowski's hands together with a towel from the kitchen. But while she was attempting to bind his hands, Frykowski began to fight back and managed to get the towel off his hands. The two then began to wrestle and ended up on the floor. Atkins managed to stab Frykowski four times in his legs and realized that she couldn't handle him, so she began to scream for help.

Watson came running and jumped on Frykowski and began to beat him on his head with the butt end of his .22 caliber rifle. Frykowski still managed to escape from Watson and went outside onto the backyard, where he began yelling for help. Watson then shot him twice, and when he fell onto the front lawn, Watson caught up with him and stabbed him fifty-one times until he stopped moving.

Frykowski was cremated and buried in Loda, Poland, at the St. Josef Cemetery.

Steve Parent

Steve Parent was the first victim of the Tate house murders. At only eighteen years old, he had lived in the Los Angeles suburb of El Monte with his parents and three siblings. Parents didn't know Roman Polanski or Sharon Tate and had never met any of the other victims who were murdered that night. Steve was also not involved with any of the Manson Family. He was simply at the wrong place at the wrong time.

Steve Parent had known the caretaker of the property, William Garretson, who lived in a cottage located at the back of the Polanski property. On the night of the murder, Parent was visiting Garretson at his cottage. While he was leaving the property after his visit, he was stopped by Tex Watson, who shot him four times.

Wilfred Parent, Steve's father, didn't like the way that the police handled his son's murder. He claimed that he was called by a detective over the phone to let him know about his son's murder, not in person. Wilfred also complained about how most of the media completely ignored the murder of his son and only talked about the more famous victims of the crime.

Steve Parent had initially met William Garretson the prior month when he was driving in Beverly Hills and Garretson was hitchhiking home. Parent stopped and picked him up, and then drove him to his place, located at the Polanski residence on Cielo Drive. The two men hit it off well, and Parent was invited back anytime.

Parent worked in electronics sales, and on Friday, August 8, 1969, he was trying to sell a Sony AM/FM Digimatic clock radio. He thought that maybe Garretson would be interested. So after work, he packed it into his car and drove out to Garretson's place around 11:30 that night. After he arrived at the cottage, Steve showed Garrettson how the clock radio worked and all its features, but he was not interested in buying it. Steve hung around for about forty-five minutes, and the two of them had a beer before he packed up the clock radio and decided to leave.

As Steve Parent approached the gate, he had to stop his vehicle, roll down his window, and press a button to open the gate. Just as he rolled down his window, Tex Watson suddenly approached the car and surprised Parent by yelling out, "Halt." When Parent saw the gun in one of Watson's hands and a buck knife in the other, he responded, "Please don't hurt me. I won't say anything."

Watson first swung his knife at Parent, missing his face but cutting the watch off his wrist as Parent had raised his arms to try to protect his face from the knife. Frustrated, Watson then shot Parent four times, quickly, killing him.

William Garretson

On the night of August 9, 1969, nineteen-year-old William Garretson, who was the caretaker of the Polanski property and lived in a small cottage at the back of the property, was unharmed and unaware of the vicious crimes that were occurring while he slept.

Garretson was born in Lancaster, Ohio, on August 24, 1949. The night of the murder, he had received a visitor around 11:30 p.m. An electronics salesman, Steve Parent, whom he had met only a month before, was trying to sell him a clock radio. After the two drank a beer and Parent left, Garretson went to bed.

It wasn't until the following morning, after the murders had been discovered, that the police searched the property and found Garretson sleeping in his bed in the cottage. Police considered him to be a prime suspect and took him into custody immediately. He was charged with suspicion of murder and interrogated by detectives.

During questioning, Garretson claimed that he heard and knew nothing of the murders. When the police broke into his place and took him into the main house to look at the bodies, he first found out about the crime that had occurred. The only body that police didn't show him was that of Sharon Tate.

Police then gave Garretson a polygraph test and declared that he was telling the truth and was clear of the murders, but his answers to what he heard showed muddy results.

Years later, during the taping of a 1990 documentary about the Manson murders at Cielo Drive, Garretson changed his story somewhat. He now said that he was listening to music after his friend Steve Parent left and heard what he thought were firecrackers going off. He believed it was the Parent throwing them out of his car window as a joke. He also said that he thought he heard a woman scream and possibly run by the pool outside the house. He thought it was a woman who was screaming because someone was throwing her into the pool. There were often late-night parties at the main house, and such gatherings were not unusual. Garretson also used drugs frequently and probably didn't want to admit this to the police.

Police could only hold Garretson for the weekend as they had no evidence to charge him with the murders, so they released him. The media followed him around and blasted his name in public to the point where he had to go into hiding. He would later sue the police, saying that they never read him his rights, thereby violating his constitutional rights. He also sued for false arrest, false imprisonment, and invasion of privacy.

The following night, while Garretson was still in police custody, the LaBianca murders happened, so he wasn't a suspect in those murders. But police never tied the two murders together at first, and different detectives from different police forces investigated them.

Garretson moved back to Lancaster, where he was from, to escape the spotlight. But he had to return on July 26, 1970, to testify at the Charles Manson trial.

Leno & Rosemary LaBianca

Leno LaBianca's parents were from Italy and owned two different grocery businesses: Gateway Ranch Markets and State Wholesale Grocery Company. Leno, along with his two sisters, all worked for their father at one of his stores. In 1940, Leno's parents purchased a new home in Los Feliz, located on Waverly Drive, a neighborhood in the upper-middle class area of Los Angeles.

After graduating from high school, Leno first attended college and then the University for Business Administration, while still working for his father. Then, in November 1943, Leno enlisted in the army, and in September 1944, he was sent to Europe to fight in World War II. Before he left for the war, he married his high school girlfriend, Alice, in March 1944.

Leno returned home after the war two years later in March 1946. He returned to working for his father, and by the Summer of 1951, he was named Vice President of both grocery chains.

At the end of 1951, Leno's father passed away, leaving him to succeed him as the company's president. Leno and his wife, along with their two children, moved into his father's house on Waverly Drive.

Over the next few years, Leno and Alice began fighting and decided to separate in January 1955. Both decided to move out of Leno's father's home on Waverly Drive and rent an apartment in Los Feliz. Alice then had the couple's third child. That didn't save their marriage, however, and they were divorced in November. Once their divorce was final, Leno sold one of the grocery chains, State Wholesale, in 1958, and focused solely on Gateway Markets.

Leno eventually met a waitress, Rosemary, and soon after, they began dating. Rosemary started her own boutique business in 1967, which became a successful, higher-end women's clothing store. The couple married in 1968, and they bought Leno's parents' old home, the place where he had grown up. Rosemary's son, Frank, from her previous marriage, moved in with them.

In the Summer of 1969, after the LaBiancas returned home from a camping trip, they were surprised to find that their dogs had escaped from the house and were running loose. When they got inside their home, they noticed some things were missing. Later, it was learned to have been one of the Manson Family's "creepy crawls," where they had broken into different homes to move things around and scare the owners.

On Saturday, July 26, 1969, Rosemary's son, Frank, went on a camping trip to Lake Isabella with one of his best friends, who was vacationing there with his family. On the following Saturday, Leno and Rosemary drove up to where the family was camping to drop off their speedboat for Frank and his friends to use. On August 9th, both Leno and Rosemary, along with her daughter, Suzan, returned to Lake Isabella to pick up Frank and the boat to bring them back home. When they arrived, Frank wanted to stay through the weekend. Rosemary said it was fine, and they loaded the boat and headed back for home.

On the way back to Los Feliz, they dropped Suzan off at her apartment in Los Angeles that evening. Next, they headed for a newspaper stand, located on Hillhurst and Franklin Streets, which Leno often frequented to get the latest copy of the *Los Angeles Herald Examiner.* Leno was a regular gambler who needed to check the horse race stats.

When they got to the newsstand, the owner told them about the big news of actress Sharon Tate and her friends being murdered at her house on Cielo Drive in Benedict Canyon. The couple was shocked, just as the rest of the city was, but they were tired and wanted to get home to bed, so they didn't hang around for very long.

They finally arrived home sometime after 1:00 a.m. on Sunday, August 10th. Rosemary went upstairs to their bedroom and got ready for bed, and Leno took the newspaper into their living room to read about what had happened in the races.

Manson and the Family were out looking for another wealthy group of people to murder, just as he did with the Tate household. He needed to create the same scene as he did before by making it look like the Black Panthers did the murders. Manson wanted to ignite the spark to set off the race war, as well as get his friend released on the murder charges of Gary Hinman. They chose the LaBianca house.

After the Manson Family broke into the LaBianca house, Charlie and Tex went into the living room where they found Leno sleeping on the couch. They woke him up and, while holding a gun pointed to his face, told him to remain quiet and nobody would get hurt. They were out looking for money and didn't want any trouble.

Manson removed a thong that he had around his neck and gave it to Tex Watson, then told him to tie LaBianca's hands behind his back. While Tex was doing this, Manson asked Leno if there were any other people in the house. He told them that his wife, Rosemary, was upstairs, probably in their bedroom.

Manson hustled up the stairs quickly and quietly, and after entering their bedroom, woke Rosemary up. She was scared and let out a loud shriek. He told her to be quiet and nobody would get hurt, then threw a dress at her, which was lying on a chair in the bedroom, and told her to put it on.

Manson then directed her downstairs and into the living room, where Tex was waiting, and he tied her up as well. Manson told them both again that nobody would be hurt if they told them where they kept any money in the house.

After they obtained the couple's money, Tex took Rosemary back upstairs and into her bedroom, where he took a pillowcase and placed it over her head. Then, he grabbed the table lamp off the end table and wrapped the power cord around her neck, pushing her onto the bed. Rosemary began to make noises and cough. Tex told her to shut up and then left the room, heading back down to the living room, only to find Manson gone.

Before Tex had time to go out to the car to look for Charlie, Leslie Van Houten and Patricia Krenwinkel came into the front door of the house and ran into him. Tex told them to go upstairs into the bedroom and keep an eye on Rosemary. After they left, Tex went back into the living room and pulled out his knife. He began to stab Leno, who started to yell and scream that he was being stabbed.

Rosemary heard her husband and got up from the bed, trying to find her way to the bedroom door. Both Krenwinkel and Van Houten attempted to wrestle her back down onto the bed to stop her from screaming. Rosemary was too powerful for the girls, and she was able to make it to the door, pulling the two of them with her as they tried to hold her down. Krenwinkel then began yelling for Tex to help them.

Tex dropped Leno onto the floor and began to run up the stairs towards the bedroom. Leno was still alive but had been stabbed so many times all over his chest and stomach, he just lay beside the sofa in pain, bleeding. When Tex went into the room and saw the two girls struggling to hold back Rosemary, he grabbed hold of the power cord, which was still hanging from Rosemary's neck, and pulled it hard. She fell to the floor. He jumped on top of her and began stabbing her, and he kept stabbing her until she stopped moving. Her autopsy would show Rosemary had forty-one stab wounds in total.

Tex ran back down the stairs and back into the living room where Leno had managed to pull himself up onto the couch. Tex jumped on Leno and began to stab him again. Once Leno stopped moving and appeared dead, he then took his knife and carved the word "War" into his stomach.

Tex then returned to the bedroom and saw Krenwinkel stabbing Rosemary with a kitchen knife. Tex looked at Van Houten and ordered her to stab Rosemary as well. Manson had told Tex that he had to make sure that everyone took part in each of the killings. Krenwinkel handed Van Houten the bloody knife, and she began stabbing Rosemary in her back and buttocks.

Later during the trial, Van Houten would claim that Rosemary was already dead when Tex forced her to stab her body. The medical report stated that Rosemary's body had been stabbed several times after she had died.

Tex went to have a shower and told the girls to write stuff on the walls. Krenwinkel wrote the words "Death to Pigs" and "Rise" on the walls and then "Helter Skelter" (misspelled) on the refrigerator door in the kitchen. She had gotten the blood by stabbing Leno in the stomach several times with a carving fork, which she just left sticking out of his stomach.

After the murders and smearing the bloody messages, they all ate some food from the kitchen and showered before leaving and hitchhiking back to Spahn Ranch.

The following night, when Frank returned home, he became scared upon noticing that all the window shades in the house were pulled down. It was never like that, so he rang the doorbell and knocked a few times. After getting no answer, he walked down the road to where there was a payphone. He called his sister Suzan, who came with her boyfriend, and they picked him up and went to their mother's house.

Suzan knew how to get in through a side door that was near the kitchen. The first thing they all saw was the phrase "Helter Skelter" written on the fridge door. While Suzan and her boyfriend were in the kitchen, Frank walked into the living room. He saw Leno tied up, bloody, and dead.

They all ran from the house and went to their next-door neighbors, who called the police. The police found Rosemary in her bedroom, dead.

The couple would be laid to rest in Los Angeles on Saturday, August 16, 1969.

Manson, Watson, Krenwinkel, and Van Houten were all later convicted of both murders. Each of them would be given the death sentence. Later, after California changed its law, the sentences were commuted to life in prison.

Donald "Shorty" Shea

Donald Shea was born in Medford, Massachusetts, on September 18, 1933. Shea decided to move out to the Los Angeles area in California with hopes of becoming an actor or movie star. Shea obtained a few small parts but nothing substantial, and he ended up working as a bouncer at several bars.

Finally, Shea found a steady job wrangling horses at the Spahn Ranch, a popular site for filming television western shows. Shea was a large man, standing at 6 feet 2 inches with a stocky build, weighing around 250 pounds. Most of the ranch hands considered Shea to be the foreman or person in charge, as he took control of everything and was constantly giving instructions to people around the ranch.

When Manson arrived at the ranch, the two men didn't get along right from the start. Manson didn't like to be given orders, and Shea could tell that he rubbed him the wrong way. Manson also didn't like that Shea was dating a black woman, Magdalene Velma Fuery, a stripper and topless dancer working under her stage name of "Nikki." When the couple got married, she stayed with Shea at the ranch, which bothered Manson.

Shea began to complain to George Spahn, owner of the ranch, that he thought the Manson group was up to no good and couldn't be trusted. He felt they should be kicked off the property. Spahn didn't want to do this because Manson was giving him different girls to have sex with regularly. So he just listened to Shea's complaints but did nothing about them.

In the early morning of August 16, 1969, over one hundred police officers raided the Spahn Ranch in search of stolen vehicles following a tip they had received. Manson blamed the raid on Shea, thinking that he had reported the tip to the police and was trying to get rid of Manson.

Police found several stolen vehicles, drugs, and other things, and Manson and several of the Family members were arrested. Three days later, when they were released, they returned to the ranch. A week later, Shea was murdered. His body wouldn't be found until December 1977.

With all the murders connected to Manson, there were several stories from different members of the Family. And they all differed. Eventually, both Steve "Clem" Grogan and Bruce Davis were arrested, charged, and convicted of Shea's murder. Grogan buried Shea's body while the other members of the Family burned, then buried all of his possessions.

One of the stories that came out about Shea's murder was from Al Springer, a member of the Straight Satan Motorcycle Club. According to Springer, when he was at the ranch one day, he was reading a newspaper story about the trial of Bobby Beausoleil, which involved another member of the Straight Satan Motorcycle Club, Danny DeCarlo. DeCarlo had turned state's evidence and was testifying for the prosecution in the case. Springer was talking with Bruce Davis and told him that he didn't like it that DeCarlo was testifying against Beausoleil. Davis responded to him, "Yes. We'll have to do something about that."

Springer replied, "That would be hard to do."

Davis responded, "We have a way of taking care of snitches," and said, "They had already taken care of one." Then he added, "We cut his arms, legs, and head off and buried him on the ranch, and the guy was a snitch." Davis said that the guy drank so much that they were afraid he was going to the police with information. So, they had to do away with him. Mark Ross, who was also present, asked, "You mean Shorty?" and Davis responded, "Yeah."

Later, while Bruce Davis was at his parole hearing, he told the parole board that Manson decided to kill Shea. Manson believed that Shea knew about the Tate and LaBianca murders and had been talking about them with other people at the Spahn Ranch, so Manson had to do what he needed to do to shut him up.

Tex Watson was later connected to Shea's murder, but he was never charged with the crime. Both Bruce Davis and Steve Grogan said that Watson was not only there when they murdered Shea, but he was the first person to stab him.

PART IV
WHO WERE THEY

Terry Melcher

Terrence P. Jorden was born on February 8, 1942, in New York City, to actress Doris Day and her husband at the time, Al Jorden. Day name Terry after her childhood appearance in the comic strip *Terry and the Pirates*. Jordan and Day were having problems with their marriage when Terry was born. The day after his birth, Day filed for divorce, claiming physical abuse. Jordan wanted her to get an abortion and not have the child, and even after she had the baby, he was never interested in spending any time with the child.

When Doris Day married her third husband, Martin Melcher, who later became her business manager and producer of many of her films, he officially adopted Terry. She changed his last name to match her husband's.

After finishing high school, Terry would go on to attend Principia College in Illinois. When Terry left college in the early 1960s, he returned to Beverly Hills and teamed up with singer Bruce Johnson to create the band Bruce & Terry. They had a few hits before deciding to form other new bands in the area.

During the 1960s, they were responsible for hit bands such as the Beach Boys and the Rip Chords, which each had several top ten hits and marked the beginning of the popular "California Surf" music genre. By the mid-1960s, Melcher began working for Columbia Records, where he continued his successful music career. He was now a producer of even more hit bands like The Byrds, Paul Revere and the Raiders, Wayne Newton, Frankie Laine, Jimmy Boyd, Pat Boone, Glen Campbell, and the Mamas & the Papas.

Dennis Wilson of the Beach Boys became good friends with Manson and even had him and his followers living with him at his home on Sunset Boulevard. While Manson was living with Wilson, he began playing his music for him and lined up an audition with the Beach Boys' record label.

Manson met Terry Melcher when he attended a party at Wilson's house, and the two discussed rock and roll all night. Melcher became very interested in Manson and invited him over to his Cielo Drive home to talk over what Manson was looking for. They set up an audition for Manson at Spahn Ranch, but Melcher never showed up due to family issues. Melcher's stepfather, Martin Melcher, died in 1968. It was then discovered that most of Doris Day's fortune, around twenty million dollars, had been mismanaged or stolen and used by Martin. The theft caused Melcher to give up renting the house located at 10050 Cielo Drive, which he shared with his girlfriend, Candace Bergen. He wanted to save his family some money, so he moved back into one of his mother's houses.

Manson, angry that Melcher hadn't shown up to his audition, went to his house on Cielo Drive, but he wasn't there. Instead, he ran into Sharon Tate and her photographer and learned that Melcher had moved, but they didn't know where he was now living.

Eventually, Manson got in touch with Melcher and set up another audition for him at Spahn Ranch. This time, he showed up and watched the whole performance. But he wasn't impressed. Instead of offering Manson a record deal, Melcher gave him some money and left.

Shortly after this, Gary Hinman was murdered by Bobby Beausoleil and arrested. Manson had to create copycat murders to try to get Beausoleil free before Beausoleil was tempted to tell what he knew.

Melcher continued producing music and was working on Jimmy Boyd's new album for A&M Records when the Tate murders happened at his old Cielo Drive address. Melcher decided it would be best to go into hiding.

Eventually, Manson and his group were arrested for the murders, and it was all over the press. Melcher's name started to come up several times during police investigations and interviews surrounding the murders. Melcher hired a bodyguard, and when Bugliosi interviewed him, he told him that he was so scared of Manson that he had also hired a psychiatrist.

Melcher returned to producing records when he helped The Byrds finish their eighth album, which was released in November 1969. He followed that with the band's subsequent two albums, which were neither commercially successful nor well-received by music reviewers. Melcher would ultimately bear most of the blame for their failures, as he had remixed the albums without the band's approval.

Melcher then became the Executive Producer for his mother, Doris Day's, new television series on *CBS'*, *The Doris Day Show*. Later in the eighties, he was the co-producer of her other television series, *Doris Day's Best Friends*.

Melcher returned to the studio to work with the Beach Boys, co-writing the song "Kokomo," which was featured in the 1988 Tom Cruise movie *Cocktail* and became the band's fourth number one hit.

Terry Melcher died of melanoma at his Beverly Hills home on November 19, 2004.

RUMORS ABOUND

According to the author of the book *Chaos: Charles Manson, the CIA, and the Secret History of the Sixties*, Tom O'Neill (click here to read the interview), claimed to have found evidence that connects Terry Melcher with Charles Manson for four months following the Tate and LaBianca murders but before Manson was charged with the murders.

O'Neill claimed that prosecutor Bugliosi had his files, which show the murders were not intended to scare Melcher because he wouldn't get Manson a record contract. But instead, O'Neill claimed to have found documents showing that Melcher was having sex with the then fifteen-year-old, Ruth Ann

Moorehouse, whose father, Dean Moorehouse, was a Manson follower living with Melcher at the Cielo Drive house. O'Neill also claimed that Tex Watson was a regular visitor at the Cielo Drive house as well.

We were easily able to unveil Melcher's relationship with Ruth Ann Moorehouse, but we're not sure how that changes anything about the murders.

Dennis Wilson

Dennis Carl Wilson was born in Inglewood, California, on December 4, 1944. He was the second of three boys born to Murray Gage Wilson and his wife, Audree Neva, who lived in Hawthorne, California. Dennis was known to be a wild child to the point where everyone in the neighborhood called him "Dennis the Menace" (after the popular television series about a boy also named Dennis who always got himself into trouble). Dennis' father was known to be very strict and not afraid to strike or belt any of the kids. Dennis later said that he got it the worst and was beaten by their dad the most.

Dennis described his brother Brian as a freak who would stay in his bedroom and listen to records instead of going out and playing sports with the rest of the kids. Dennis was into cars and girls, but the three brothers would often practice singing songs in their shared bedroom, usually later on in the night. These late-night sessions were when they learned to harmonize well with each other.

Dennis started taking drum lessons in 1960, and his mother forced Brian to include Dennis in his new band called the Beach Boys. They would officially become a band in the Fall of 1961, and their father, Murray, decided to manage them. It was Dennis' idea to create music centered on the West Coast California surfing community, even though he was the only one in the band who surfed. He encouraged Brian to write a song about it, which ultimately became known as "Surfin'." It soon became a local hit and was even played on the local radio station.

In 1963, Dennis joined with Gary Usher, and the two of them released a single, "RPM." By March 1964, he bought his own home in Hollywood and moved out of the family house. The band released their next album in the Summer of 1964, called *All Summer Long*.

Dennis began to experience financial difficulties, primarily due to his struggle managing his finances.

His father told a newspaper reporter in December 1964 that Dennis was "crying because he had spent all his money." Besides paying $25,000 on his new home, the rest just seemed to disappear.

When the Beach Boys were on stage, Dennis received more attention from the girls than Brian, who was the lead singer and writer of most of the songs. Brain told the band in January 1965 that he wasn't going to do any more live shows with the band because Dennis got more attention. Dennis later said that he thought Brian was the Beach Boys, and that they were just his messengers. He felt that Brian was the whole band, and the rest of them were nothing.

Their next album, *The Beach Boys Today*, released in March 1965, had Dennis singing the lead on a couple of tracks for the first time. One of the songs, "Do You Wanna Dance," made it to number 12 on the Billboard Charts.

The following year, Dennis began using drugs such as LSD more often, and he started becoming irregular in showing up for band rehearsals. Brian began recording the next album, *Pet Sounds*, using a session drummer named Hal Blaine. Dennis ended up only playing on one track for that album, "That's Not Me."

By 1968, Dennis began writing songs for the band, which would be recorded and included on their albums. On April 6th, during one of these recording sessions, Dennis was driving home when he saw two cute girls, Patricia Krenwinkel and Leslie Van Houten, standing on the roadside hitchhiking. He pulled over and offered them a ride. They agreed and got into the car. He took them to the ranch where they lived and dropped them off.

Less than a week later, on April 11th, Dennis saw the two girls out hitchhiking again. He pulled over and asked them where they were heading, and they told him nowhere really. Dennis told them to get in and come back to his house, where they could have some milk and cookies.

When they returned to Dennis' house, he brought them each a glass of milk and a plate of cookies, and they were surprised, beginning to laugh. They admitted that they didn't believe him about the milk and cookies and thought they were going to his place to have sex or something like that. During their conversations, Dennis mentioned that he was into the Maharishi, and so they told him about a spiritual guru named Charlie, with whom they lived.

Later that night, Wilson had to attend a recording session for his band and gave the girls a ride to their place. When they saw Charlie, he asked them who had given them a ride home because he was driving a nice car. They told him it was a guy named Dennis who belonged to a band called the Beach Boys, which they had never heard of before.

Charlie recognized the name immediately and became suddenly interested. He told them to get in the car and lead the way to Dennis' house. Manson also had several other Family members take cars and follow them there.

Later that night, when Dennis finished with his recording session, he headed home. The studio was located at the back of his property, so he didn't have far to go. When he pulled up to the house, he saw this short, hairy man with a beard standing outside his door. Wilson's first question to the man was, "Are you going to hurt me?" Manson laughed and led him into his own house. Inside, there were more than a dozen people, mostly women, most of them naked and stoned, listening to a Beatles album.

Throughout that first night, Manson and Wilson got along wonderfully. Smoking pot and talking music, Love, and all things fun. Before he knew it, Manson had invited himself and the rest of his followers to come and live there with Wilson.

According to Wilson, over the next six months, it would cost him around one hundred grand to take care of Manson's Family in food, drink, and other supplies, which included penicillin injections because many of the girls would keep picking up STDs while they were camped out at his house. Despite the cost, Wilson was thrilled to have them there. He started to idolize Manson, to the point where, during an interview with *Rave Magazine*, he told them about a new guy the band was going to record with on their latest record label, who was a "Wizard."

When Manson tried recording for the Beach Boys' label, their manager wasn't impressed. He then recorded some of his music in Dennis's studio as well. Then Wilson introduced Manson to producer Terry Melcher, who had a string of hits throughout the 1960s. Manson auditioned for Melcher at Spahn Ranch as well, and Melcher quietly introduced him to a music manager he knew, hoping that he would find Manson a label that might record him.

As 1968 continued, Dennis decided to use one of Manson's songs, "Cease to Exist," for the B-side of one of their singles. Only Wilson made a few musical changes and also changed some of the words and the title of the song to "Never Learn Not to Love." Not only did he do this without asking Manson, but he also didn't list him as one of the songwriters. In Dennis' mind, Manson owed him one hundred thousand dollars for taking care of him and his Family for six months.

Wilson decided to give up his house while he went on tour in Europe, so he told Manson that he and his Family would have to leave and find somewhere else to live. Manson initially moved into record manager Gregg Jakobson's house and lived in his basement. The Family remained in Wilson's house, selling off all of his furniture and possessions that were left there to pay for their food and survival. The house owner eventually evicted them.

In August 1969, after the Tate and LaBianca murders occurred, Manson showed up at Wilson's new place and told him that he had been to the moon and back. He then asked Wilson for some money, and Wilson gave him all that he had on him at the time.

In November that year, after Manson's arrest for the murders made the press, Dennis told prosecutor Bugliosi that he couldn't testify against him because he was too frightened of him and his followers. He told Bugliosi that someone had left a bullet outside his balcony door. Bugliosi decided that he could take a sworn statement from Wilson, and if he obtained a corroborating witness, which he did, Gregg Jakobson, he wouldn't need Wilson to testify.

Bugliosi also requested some of the recordings Wilson had made with Manson for the trial. Still, Wilson told him that he had destroyed them all because the vibrations connected to those songs didn't belong on this Earth anymore.

By this time, everyone who knew Wilson was worried about his mental stability as he was taking heavy amounts of drugs and was feeling guilty for bringing Manson into the music world.

Throughout the 1970s, Wilson continued to get death threats over the phone, which he thought were coming from Manson Family members. In 1978, the biography *The Beach Boys and the California Myth* had a section where Wilson said, "I know why Manson did what he did and someday, I'll tell the world. I'll write a book and explain why he did it."

His biographer, Mark Dillon, later explained how Wilson had spiraled into a self-destructive lifestyle because of his drug intake and feeling of guilt for introducing Manson to many of his friends.

The Beach Boys informed Dennis Wilson that he would have to undergo rehab after a performance they gave in September 1983, or he would be banned from playing live with them again. At this time, he was homeless and was living from one friend's couch to another.

Wilson checked into St. John's Hospital in Santa Monica on December 23, 1983, but stayed there for only two nights. On the night of December 25th, he got into a violent fight at the Santa Monica Hotel and then went to a different hospital in Santa Monica.

A few days later, on December 28th, Dennis drowned in Marina Del Rey. After spending the day drinking, he decided to start diving into the water to try and find items that had belonged to his ex-wife that he had thrown into the water three years prior while they were going through their divorce. The medical report stated that Wilson had probably experienced shallow water blackout before dying.

He was buried at sea on January 4, 1984, by the U.S. Coast Guard.

RUMORS ABOUND

Mike Love, Dennis Wilson's cousin and a member of the Beach Boys, wrote his memoir in 2016. In that book, Love claimed that Wilson once told him that he saw Manson shoot a black man in half with an M16 rifle, and afterwards, he hid the body inside a wall.

Terry Melcher also claimed that Wilson knew that Manson had been killing people, and it freaked him out. He thought that he should maybe tell the cops, only he was too scared to.

Carole Freedman later told author Tom O'Neill that many stars in the Hollywood community had a closer association with Manson than has been reported in public.

Roman Polanski

On August 18, 1933, Roman Polanski was born in
Paris, France. His father was Bula Katz-
Przedborska, who later, after World War II, became
known as Ryszard Polanski. Roman's father was
originally from Poland, and his mother was Mojzesz
Liebling, from Russia.

In 1937, the Polanskis moved back to Poland to a
town named Kraków. Two years later, when the
Nazis invaded Poland, they were still living there,
and they were forced to move into the ghetto part
of town by the German Army along with the Jews
and other outcasts. Roman was only able to study
for a few weeks in school before all the Jews were
expelled and no longer allowed to enter a classroom
in Poland.

Roman watched his father be lined up with hundreds of other Jews from his town as they were being sent to German concentration camps in Mauthausen. Roman didn't understand what was going on, so he snuck around the lines of prisoners to try and find out what he was supposed to do. When his father saw him, knowing that he would only be hurt if the Nazis spotted him, he told him to get away and hide.

When Roman returned to their home, he learned that his mother, who was about four months pregnant, had been taken away. She was sent to Auschwitz and died in the gas chamber there. Roman's father had a friend, Stefania Buchala, who promised to help take care of Roman and, in 1943, assisted him in escaping the country.

Polanski had a fascination with film and movies since childhood. Even at the age of four, he would find himself mesmerized by watching any film he could. At that time, the only movies he saw were the German newsreels shown in the open markets.

After the war ended, he began to watch movies that were presented in theaters or at schools. The 1947 film *Odd Man Out*, by Carol Reed, is still considered one of the best movies ever made and had a significant influence on his subsequent film creations.

In the early 1950s, Polanski relocated to the city of Łódź to attend the National Film School of Łódź. He acted in two different films that were made there before directing his first film, a short film called *Rower*. Polanski would go on to make two full-length films before graduating in 1959. Also in 1959, Polanski married Barbara Kwiatkowska-Lass, one of the actresses who starred in the short film *When Angels Fall*, which Polanski directed while in school. The couple separated only one year after and were soon divorced.

In 1962, Polanski made his first film to be widely released, *Knife in the Water*, which became a hit in the West and earned him an Oscar nomination for Best Foreign Language Film the following year. The Oscar nomination also gave Polanski a name in the international film community.

Polanski moved to France to continue his film career, but at that time, France was very xenophobic, so he moved to England. While there, he made two psychological horror films, *Repulsion* and *Cul-de-sac*, which were popular at the time.

In 1967, Polanski made *Fearless Vampire Killers*, a parody of the current vampire and monster horror films, which were all the rage. It was his first full-length feature film made in color. During the film, Polanski met and got to know actress Sharon Tate, who had come from the United States. The couple married one year later on January 20, 1968.

Polanski began working for Paramount Studios and was sent to the United States to direct his next film, *Downhill Racer*. While there, he was given Ira Levin's novel *Rosemary's Baby*, which he loved. In only three weeks, Polanski had written a 272-page screenplay for the book and would go on to direct the movie as well. The film became a box office smash, making him the newest major filmmaker of the time.

Polanski and Tate rented a home at 10050 Cielo Drive, located in the Benedict Canyon area of Los Angeles. Both Polanski and Tate were off to different parts of Europe, each going to work on a film. Tate finished her work first and flew back home, which was a relief for her, as she was now eight months pregnant.

When they were both gone, they had Polanski's childhood friend, Wojciech Frykowski, and his girlfriend, Abigail Folger, staying at the house to take care of things there. When Tate returned home, they decided to continue visiting until Polanski got back home.

The night of August 8th, the Manson Family found their way into the Cielo Drive home and murdered Sharon Tate, her unborn baby who was already named Paul Richard Polanski, as well as her two friends who were staying with her, Frykowski and Folger, another friend Jay Sebring, and a young visitor, Steven Parent, to the Cielo Drive property caretaker that same evening.

Polanski returned home from Europe the next day and had to identify his wife's body. He placed a $25,000 reward out for the arrest of her murderers. The press was reporting salacious stories about Tate and the rest of their friends, which told of them having Satanic parties and doing lots of drugs. Everything had turned into tabloid journalism. Later, Polanski said that he couldn't believe what he was seeing. The press was blaming the victims for their murders.

Polanski returned to filmmaking in 1971 with *Macbeth,* followed by the award-winning *Chinatown* and numerous other notable films. In 1979, he would finally make *Tess,* which he had planned to have Tate star in after she had told him to read the story. He dedicated this movie to her.

Polanski was arrested in 1977 when he was charged with sex offenses, including drugging and raping a thirteen-year-old girl, Samantha Gailey. This assault was supposed to have happened while Polanski was doing a photo shoot with Gainey at Jack

Nicholson's house. During his arraignment, he pleaded not guilty to all charges.

Gailey's attorney arranged a plea bargain that would eliminate five of the charges, which Polanski agreed to. He had to plead guilty to one charge of unlawful sexual intercourse with a minor. He had to undergo a ninety-day psychiatric evaluation at the California Institute for Men. Polanski was also placed on probation.

Through the grapevine, Polanski heard that the judge who was to preside over his case, Laurence J. Rittenband, had told screenwriter Howard E. Koch, one of Polanski's friends, that he was not going to accept the plea bargain. Instead, he was going to send Polanski to prison for fifty years and make sure that he never got out of prison. Gailey's attorney confirmed this.

Polanski decided not to attend his sentencing. He flew to London, where he already owned a house, on January 31, 1978. He gathered up some essential things and the following day flew to Paris. He was still a French citizen, which protected him from being extradited to the United States, so he took up full-time residence there.

The following year, Polanski was interviewed by author Martin Amis, and his comments sparked considerable controversy. "If I had killed someone, there wouldn't have been so much press reporting on it. But because it involved fucking, you see, and to young girls, there was lots. Judges want to fuck young girls. Juries want to fuck young girls. Actually, everyone wants to fuck young girls."

About ten years later, Gailey sued Polanski in civil court. She was not only suing for the sexual assault, but also false imprisonment, seduction of a minor, and intentional infliction of emotional distress. After eight years of litigation, in 1997, Polanski settled with Gailey.

In March 2023, Gailey and her new husband met Polanski, along with his new wife, in France for a magazine cover story. In that story, Gailey would say, "Let me be clear, what happened with Polanski was never a big problem for me. I didn't even know it was illegal. I didn't know someone could be arrested for it. I was fine. I'm still fine. It was so unfair and completely unjust. Everyone should know by now that Roman has served his sentence, which, in my opinion, was long. Anyone who thinks he deserves to be in prison is wrong. It isn't the case today, and it wasn't the case yesterday."

PART V
THE MANSON FAMILY

Bobby Beausoleil

Robert "Bobby" Beausoleil was born to a middle-class family on November 6, 1947, and grew up in Santa Barbara, California. He frequently got into legal trouble for minor crimes, and by the time he was fifteen, he was sent to a reform school for ten months. After he was released in early 1964, he didn't return home. Instead, he became a transient, moving between San Francisco and Los Angeles. He joined rock bands and acted in local theaters until 1966, when he met Gary Hinman and joined his band, Milky Way.

Beausoleil met Charles Manson at the band's first practice, as he was also a member of the band. Manson was recently released from prison earlier that year and was living in Topanga Canyon.

The following year, in 1967, he met filmmaker Kenneth Anger and appeared in his film *Lucifer Rising*. After he completed his work on the film, Beausoleil moved into Gary Hinman's house in Topanga Canyon. While living there, he began meeting other members of Manson's Family, usually the female ones.

Hinman was believed to have inherited approximately $20,000, and after Manson heard this, he began sending his girls over to try to convince Hinman to move to Spahn Ranch with them. Manson even made a few visits to Hinman's house to try to convince him how much better his life would be if he came to join the commune. But Hinman wouldn't budge. He loved his life the way it was.

Manson decided that he could no longer wait to get Hinman's money. There was the pressure of Helter Skelter looming, and they needed the money to make their move to the desert and prepare for the race war. He told Beausoleil to get the cash from Hinman and take Susan Atkins and Mary Brunner with him.

The three of them arrived at the house just as they had gone out there before. Hinman let them in and offered them all drinks. Soon, Beausoleil became aggressive and told Hinman that they wanted the money. It's not precisely clear whether they asked for drug money or more, such as the twenty thousand dollars in inheritance, as different stories were told. After several hours of trying and even using force, Beausoleil was unable to get the money from Hinman, so he called Manson.

Manson showed up with Bruce Davis, and when Hinman answered the door, Manson took his sword and sliced the left side of his face, almost completely cutting off his ear. They dragged him back into the house, and while Manson threatened him, Davis was roughing him up. Manson and Davis decided to leave, but on his way out, Manson told Beausoleil, "You know what to do."

After Manson was gone, Beausoleil decided to try to sew up Hinman's ear with some dental floss he had lying around. Over the next three days, Beausoleil tried to force Hinman to give him the money by using force, hitting him, and even torture.

Beausoleil finally called Manson again. This time, he was told not only to murder Hinman, but to make sure that they left the house looking like the murder was done by the Black Panthers. He told Beausoleil to leave a panther paw print on

Hinman's wall by sticking the palm of his hand in some of Hinman's blood and pressing it against the wall. Then Manson told him to take his finger and draw three panther prints on the wall as well, also with Hinman's blood.

Beausoleil kept stabbing Hinman until he tired. It seemed like no matter how many times he was stabbed, he wouldn't die. So, in between each attack that Beausoleil did, Atkins and Brunner would take turns sitting on top of him and holding a pillow over his face to try to suffocate him.

When Hinman finally died, Beausoleil did as Charlie told him. Using Hinman's blood, he created a panther-like paw print on the living room wall. The girls, it's questionable exactly who, wrote "Political Piggie" on the wall as well. In Manson's thinking, "piggie" was what Blacks called the police at the time as a slur. But what he didn't realize was that most of the war protesters and revolutionaries also called the police "piggies" as well. In Manson's mind, having both the paw print and the word piggie would make police think that it was the Black Panthers who did the murder. He was wrong.

Before they murdered Hinman, Beausoleil forced Hinman to sign over both of his vehicles to him. The girls took one of the cars back to Spahn Ranch while Beausoleil took the other. On August 6th, while Beausoleil was out joyriding in Hinman's Fiat, he got tired. So he pulled the car over and went to sleep. A few hours later, a police cruiser saw the car parked and stopped to ensure the driver was okay. Once they ran the license plate, they discovered that it was stolen. They arrested Beausoleil and searched the vehicle. They found the knife, which had been used to murder Hinman, stuck in the tire well of the car.

On April 18, 1970, Beausoleil was convicted of murdering Gary Hinman in the first-degree and sentenced to the death penalty. Just as in the other murder cases tried before 1972 in California, all death sentences were commuted to life imprisonment.

Years later, while Beausoleil was giving an interview, he told the reporter a different scenario about the Gary Hinman murder. According to Beausoleil, he had conducted a drug deal with the biker gang, "The Straight Satans." He said he had met several of their members who would hang out at the ranch and party. Hinman was making mescaline out at his Topanga house, so it was perfect. Beausoleil would get the money from the biker gang, bring it to Hinman, pick up the drugs, return to the ranch, and give it to the gang. He could also take a bit of the drugs for himself and get a commission for the sale. Only the last time, when he brokered the deal and brought the drugs back to the bikers, they complained that the drugs were not good or there was something wrong with them after some of the guys who used them got sick.

He now claimed that this was the reason that he went, along with Atkins and Brunner, to Hinman's house. It was to get the drug money back for the Straight Satans for the harmful drugs that he had sold to them. He also said that Manson had never come to the house that night, and it was he who cut Hinman's ear, which happened by accident while they were struggling over a gun.

This story was never mentioned before by anyone, even during the trial. Even when Susan Atkins was asked about the drug-dealing tale, she said that she had never heard that before.

In 1972, the famous author Truman Capote interviewed Bobby Beausoleil while he was in San Quentin Prison. The interview was published as a short story in 1980 and was called "Then it all Came Down" in his book *Music for Chameleons*. Beausoleil complained about the writing, saying that much of it was false and that Capote took gross literary license. Capote's biographer responded by saying that Capote rarely took actual notes when conducting these kinds of interviews and relied on his memory, which had been proven to be fallible in the past.

Then It All Came Down: Truman Capote Interviews Bobby Beausoleil. San Quentin, 1973. | Truman Capote

---

Beausoleil was transferred from San Quentin to the Oregon State Penitentiary located in Salem, Oregon, in 1994. While he was serving time there, he met a woman who lived in Oregon, and the couple had four children together. Beausoleil was transferred again in the Summer of 2015 to the Deuel Vocational Institute, located in Tracy, California.

After several times being denied for parole, Beausoleil finally got approved in January 2019, citing that he was only twenty years old when he committed the murder and should have been tried as a young offender. He had also had an excellent record while serving his time in prison. The prosecution office disagreed with the parole board's decision. By April 26, 2019, California Governor

Gavin Newsom overturned the parole board's approval.

More recently, in January 2025, the parole board again approved Beausoleil for parole. However, as of this writing, Governor Newsom has not yet decided on the matter.

Tex Watson

Charles Denton Watson was the youngest of three children born in Dallas, Texas, on December 2, 1945. He grew up close to Copeville and was not only an honor student in high school but also the editor of the school newspaper and captain of the football team. His family attended church regularly. In the Fall of 1964, he moved to Denton, Texas, to attend the University of North Texas.

Watson worked as a baggage handler at Braniff International, where he got free airline tickets to travel. On one of his trips, he flew to Los Angeles to visit one of his old fraternity brothers from university. While there, he was introduced to psychedelic drugs and hung out around the beach.

One day, when he was driving home from the beach, he picked up a hitchhiker who turned out to be Dennis Wilson, the Beach Boys' drummer. When they arrived at Wilson's house, Dennis invited him in for a drink. That's when he met Manson and a few of the Family members. At that time, they were already living with Wilson.

Watson eventually moved to Spahn Ranch with the Family when they left Wilson's home. During his time there, he started to believe in Manson's stories about the upcoming race war and that he was to take over, ruling the world after the Blacks defeated all the whites except them.

Sometime in December 1968, Watson left the Family at Spahn Ranch and moved in with a lover who had an apartment in Hollywood. They sold small amounts of drugs to survive. After only a few months, he decided to leave her and go back to Spahn Ranch.

After his return to the Family, Manson was telling his followers that they needed to get money so they could move out to the desert and hide away from the race war. Watson remembered a friend, Bernard Crowe, with whom he lived in Hollywood, and his lover. Eventually, Manson and Watson went to see Crowe, and after a brief fight, Manson shot Crowe in the stomach and left, thinking that he was dead.

Watson would later use that same weapon in the Tate murders.

On August 9, 1969, Charles Tex Watson led three of the Manson Family girls, Susan Atkins, Linda Kasabian, and Patricia Krenwinkel, to the home of Roman Polanski and Sharon Tate located at 10050 Cielo Drive where they murdered four people who were in the house: Sharon Tate, Jay Sebring, Abigail Folger, and Fry Wykowski, and a fifth person outside of the house, Steven Parent.

On the following night of August 10th, Watson, along with Patricia Krenwinkel and Leslie Van Houten, went out again to the home of Leno and Rosemary LaBianca on Waverly Drive, Los Feliz, and murdered both occupants. On this trip, Manson accompanied them to ensure everything was done correctly, but left before anyone was murdered.

Two months later, on October 2, 1969, Watson left Spahn Ranch and returned to Texas, evading the law that was now searching for him. Months later, he was found and arrested for the murders and extradited to California.

On October 12, 1971, Watson was convicted of seven charges of first-degree murder: Sharon Tate, Abigail Folger, Jay Sebring, Wojciech Frykowski, Steven Parent, Leno LaBianca, Rosemary LaBianca, and one charge of conspiracy to commit murder. A week later, the jury sentenced him to death in the gas chamber. Watson avoided execution, though, after the California Supreme Court voided all death sentences that had been imposed before 1972.

Watson's autobiography, *Will You Die for Me?*, written by Raymond Hoekstra, was published in 1978.

Watson married Kristin Joan Svege, and the couple founded Abounding Love Ministries in 1980, as they were both Christians. Watson had converted back to Christianity in 1975 and was ordained as a minister in 1981. The couple were permitted to have conjugal visits and had three sons and one daughter.

However, in 1996, prisoners who were convicted of crimes and had been given a life sentence were no longer permitted to have conjugal visits with their spouses. The pair were divorced in 2003 after being married for twenty-four years. In that same year, Svege remarried. Watson and Svege have remained friends. Watson continued to take courses and study, and in 2009, he achieved a B.A. in Business Management.

Watson's attorney, Bill Boyd, died, and his law firm went into bankruptcy. While Watson was being tried for the murders, Boyd made several recordings with him, and now these recordings have become part of the bankruptcy proceedings. Watson didn't want these tapes released to the public, but when he went to court, the judge ruled that Watson had waived his attorney-client privilege by allowing his autobiographer to hear the recording while writing the book. Eventually, the LAPD gained possession of the tapes, which are reported to have Watson confessing to the murders, but offered no new information.

In 2014, Leslie Van Houten's lawyer subpoenaed the recording to be used for her parole hearings.

Watson first became eligible for parole on November 26, 1976, but his request was denied. During his first hearing, a petition was submitted that had over 80,000 signatures from people who opposed Watson's release from prison.

In the 1980s, Sharon Tate's mother, Doris, was behind the group "Citizens for Truth," which gathered signatures for the petition. Years later, her other two daughters, Patricia and Debra, drove the petitions, which saw the signature base grow to around two million.

Watson has been denied parole eighteen more times since then. He remains locked up in San Diego County at the Richard J. Donovan Correctional Facility.

In 2023, Watson began producing a podcast of sermons delivered from 1977 to 1984 at the California Men's Colony.

Bruce Davis

On December 2, 1970, Bruce Davis was the final member of the Manson Family to go on trial for the murder of Gary Hinman and Donald "Shorty" Shea. David had a strong interest in Scientology and hit it off right away with Manson. He joined the Manson Family in 1967.

Bruce Davis was born in Monroe, Louisiana, on October 5, 1942, and grew up in Mobile, Alabama. He attempted college in Tennessee but dropped out after just one semester. In 1962, he headed to California and got a job in construction, becoming deeply immersed in the new hippie culture that was prevalent at the time.

One story about the Gary Hinman murder was that after Beausoleil was unable to get any money out of Hinman, he phoned Manson and told him that Hinman was holding out. Manson headed out to Himan's house, accompanied by Bruce Davis. Davis was a witness to Manson slicing off Hinman's ear and hearing Manson order the murder of Hinman directed at Beausoleil before Davis and Manson left.

Bruce Davis's account of what happened in the Donald Shea murder is as follows:

"We were at the ranch early in the morning. Manson came down and said, "We're going to kill Shorty." I said, "What for?" "Well, he's a snitch." Charlie is there. Bill Bass is there. He says, "You guys take him. Ask him to take you down the hill to get some car parts and kill him on the way down the hill." I was in the car when Steve Grogan hit Shorty with the pipe wrench. Charles Watson stabbed him. I was in the back seat with...with Grogan.

They took Shorty out. They had to go down the hill to a place. I stayed in the car for quite a while, but what...then I went down the mountain later, and that's when I cut Shorty on the shoulder with the knife after he was...

well, I don't know if he was dead or not. He didn't bleed when I cut him on the shoulder.

And I...I did touch Shorty Shea with a machete on the back of his neck. Didn't break the skin. I mean, I couldn't do it. And then I threw the knife, and he handed me a bayonet, and it...I just reached over, and I don't know which side it was on, but I cut him right about here on the shoulder, just with the tip of the blade. Sort of like saying, "Are you satisfied, Charlie?" And I turned around and walked away. And I...I was sick for about two or three days. I mean, I couldn't even think about what I...what I had done."

Davis is serving two life sentences for the murders of Gary Hinman and Donald Shea. He had been up for parole several times, and each time he was approved. However, it was always reversed by the Governor of California.

Davis has become a born-again Christian and earned a doctorate in Philosophy and Religion, ministering to the other inmates. He was also married and fathered a child while still being in prison at the San Luis Obispo, California Men's Colony.

In a 2017 documentary entitled *Manson Speaks: Inside the Mind of a Madman*, Detective Cliff Shepard posited that Bruce Davis might have been involved in the deaths known among Mansonites as "The Retaliation Murders." These deaths included Manson Family member John Haught, a.k.a. Christopher Zero, Sandra Good's boyfriend Joel Pugh, Attorney Ronald Hughes, and Reet Jurvetson. Of course, being a fifty-year-old case, Shepard failed to turn up any objective evidence of Davis' involvement. Indeed, though, some strange and compelling facts suggest there's more to the story.

Steve "Clem" Grogan

Steve Grogan was born in Los Angeles on July 13, 1951, and had a difficult childhood, dropping out of school as a young teenager. His parents were frustrated and let him go live and work at the Spahn Ranch, hoping that it would help him. This was long before the Manson Family went to live there.

Donald Shea, who ran the ranch, liked him and protected him, as most of the others at the ranch considered him unintelligent and nicknamed him "Scramblehead."

On the night of August 10, 1969, Grogan rode along when members of the Manson Family—Tex Watson, Patricia Krenwinkel, and Leslie Van Houten—were dropped off at Leno and Rosemary

LaBianca's house. Manson, Grogan, Susan Atkins, and Linda Kasabian continued to Venice Beach.

After arriving at the beach, Manson sent Grogan, Atkins, and Kasabian to kill actor Saladin Nader. Kasabian didn't want to be involved in another murder and took them all to the wrong apartment. After realizing that they had the wrong place, they gave up and went back home.

Grogan would later be involved with the murder of Donald Shea with Manson and Bruce Davis. The three were charged and convicted, with Manson and Davis both getting life sentences while Grogan received the death penalty. Later, a judge would commute Grogan's sentence to life as he considered Grogan to be too stupid to have decided anything on his own.

Years later, Grogan helped authorities find Shea's remains by drawing them a map. He had learned the details from Manson while they were serving time together. His help in finding the body benefited Grogan in getting parole on November 11, 1985.

Grogan met a woman while serving time and was allowed conjugal visits, during which the couple had two children. He is now living in Northern California with his family.

Leslie Van Houten (Lulu)

Leslie Van Houten was born in Los Angeles, California, to her auctioneer father, Paul Van Houten, and schoolteacher mother, Jane Edwards, on August 23, 1949. She had one older brother, Paul, and her parents also adopted two younger orphans, one boy and one girl, both from Korea. The family lived together in Altadena, a middle-class suburb of Los Angeles. By the time Leslie turned fourteen, her parents had divorced. Leslie then lived with her mother.

At the age of fifteen, Leslie began to use drugs like marijuana and LSD and was often skipping school, going out to parties, and meeting up with boys. After she met Robert Mackie, the two began dating. She became pregnant at the age of fifteen. Leslie later claimed that her mother forced her to have an abortion and bury the remains in the backyard where they lived. From that time, Leslie was no longer close to her mother and slowly drifted into a hippie commune lifestyle.

At the age of seventeen, Leslie decided to run away with her boyfriend at the time, but she returned a few months later so she could complete high school in 1967. After that, she enrolled in a secretarial school and joined the Self-Realization Fellowship group, which studies spirituality through yoga. She became a nun for the group.

Only a year later, Leslie became bored with her new lifestyle as a nun and decided to leave the group and travel around the country. While in California, she met a musician named Bobby Beausoleil, and they began a romantic relationship. One of Bobby's friends, Catherine Share, told her about a great Family run by Charlie Manson, so Leslie went to meet him and became a follower quickly afterwards.

After Leslie began to live with the Manson Family, she claimed that she became "saturated in acid" and was unable to understand the difference between real life and a psychedelic one. Leslie was never as close to Manson as many of the other girls, and Manson always referred to her as one of Bobby's girls.

Van Houten joined Manson, Tex Watson, and Patricia Krenwinkel on the night of August 10, 1969. Leslie said she wasn't aware of what was going to happen that evening, but felt that she had to go along with it and, hopefully, Manson would be more accepting of her.

Once they arrived at the LaBianca house on Waverly Drive, Charlie and Tex left the girls in the car while they went into the house. After a while, Charlie returned and told the girls to go into the house through the front door and follow Tex's instructions.

After they both entered the house, Tex instructed them to go upstairs to the bedroom and attend to the women there. Once they got to the room, they saw Rosemary LaBianca lying on the bed with her hands tied behind her back and a pillowcase placed over her head with the power cord of the table lamp tied around her neck.

Leslie and Krenwinkel remained still as neither of them knew what they were supposed to be doing. The tied and gagged woman was still alive as she was moving around on the bed and moaning. Suddenly, they all heard loud yelling from two men coming down the stairs. "No! Stop stabbing me! They're killing me!"

Instantly, Rosemary got herself up off the bed and began trying to find her way to the bedroom door. She also began to answer her husband, yelling that she was on her way. Both Leslie and Krenwinkel grabbed Rosemary, but even together, they weren't strong enough to pull her down or stop her from going for the door. Krenwinkel then began to scream for help from Tex.

Minutes later, Tex burst into the room to see both girls trying to hold on to Rosemary as she made her way around the room, even though she was still tied and had the pillowcase over her face. Tex walked right over to the three women and pushed hard on them, causing both Leslie and Krenwinkel to fall to the ground.

Rosemary somehow managed to remain standing and started moving towards the door again. Tex grabbed the cord, which was hanging from her neck, and pulled it hard until she fell to the ground. He then jumped on her, pulled out his knife, and began stabbing her.

Krenwinkel got up and walked over to Tex and Rosemary, got down on her knees, and began to stab Rosemary as well. Leslie just stood there in shock, watching and saying nothing. Before long,

Rosemary stopped moving or making any noises. Tex and Krenwinkel both stood up and began to wipe the blood that had splashed onto their faces.

Tex remembered that Manson had ordered him to make sure that everyone took part in the murders, so he handed his bloody knife to Leslie and told her to stab the bitch. Leslie knelt on one knee and looked at Rosemary, who was now lying on her stomach, but didn't move. Tex then let out a loud yell, "Fucking do it, now!"

Out of fear, Leslie began stabbing without looking at the woman. She ended up stabbing Rosemary sixteen times in her lower back and buttock areas. Later, when testifying, she said she couldn't tell if Rosemary was still alive when she was stabbing her. There was no way for her to tell, she said. The medical exam showed that Rosemary had been stabbed several times after she was already dead.

After Manson and the Family had been arrested and she was charged with the LaBianca murders, the court assigned her an attorney, Donald Barnett. A few weeks later, Manson got into an argument with Barnett, and Leslie fired him.

The court assigned her a second attorney, Marvin Part, who wanted to declare that Leslie was insane and that was the reason she was involved in the murders. Leslie and Part began arguing over this as she didn't think that she was insane.

During the trial, when Part was questioning a doctor about how LSD affected someone, the doctor began answering that the person using the drug could easily be controlled. Leslie yelled out to the court, "That's a big lie! The only thing that influenced me was the Vietnam War on TV." Leslie then fired Part.

The court appointed her a third attorney, Ronald Hughes, who argued to the court that Leslie's capacity for any rational thought had been diminished because of the amount of LSD she had been using. He also claimed that she had to obey the orders to commit these murders from Manson, who had a significant influence over her at the time.

The jury took into account the fact that Leslie was constantly giggling and smiling in court throughout the trial. When she testified, she admitted to murdering the two victims but told the court that Charlie had nothing to do with them and that he didn't tell her to murder anybody.

Leslie was convicted of murder along with the other Family members who were charged in this trial, Manson, and Krenwinkel. During the sentencing part, Leslie was sent for a psychiatric evaluation. She told the psychiatrist that she was involved in another murder, which Charlie had nothing to do with. Even though Leslie was never engaged in this other murder, she wanted the psychiatrist to believe that she was capable of murdering somebody on her own.

During the sentencing phase of the trial, Ronald Hughes wanted to show that Leslie had remorse for the murders. In front of the jury, he asked her if she felt sorry for her actions in the murder, and Leslie answered by saying, "Sorry is only a five-letter word, and you can't undo something that is done."

Leslie then went on by telling the court, "I stabbed her of my own free will. Charlie had nothing to do with it." Hughes then asked her if she could tell if Rosemary was still alive when she stabbed her. "Of course she was, I could feel her moving around as I was stabbing her in the spine, and she would let out screams." The autopsy showed that Rosemary had been stabbed several times after she was already dead. Krenwinkel and/or Leslie probably inflicted these wounds, but it couldn't be determined.

Before the sentence was handed down, Hughes went missing and was later found dead. Leslie was sentenced to death, which made her not only the youngest ever to be sentenced to death, but also the first woman. The prison had to build a death row for females, as they had never needed one before.

The California Institute for Women built a special unit for the killer females. Leslie Van Houten, Patricia Krenwinkel, and Susan Atkins were all housed there, but kept apart from the general prison population. Later in 1975, all three women were moved to the general population part of the prison.

The 1972 Supreme Court decision resulted in all previously imposed death sentences being commuted to life in prison. Leslie's sentence was automatically changed to life in prison, and she became eligible for parole after seven years of serving.

By 1978, Leslie was eligible to apply for parole, and if granted, she would have been released. The Governors didn't gain the power to rescind paroles they disagreed with until 1988.

One year before Leslie was up for her first parole hearing in 1977, her conviction was overturned because the court that initially tried her should have called a mistrial when her attorney was found dead. As well, the jury foreman of her trial told reporters that they couldn't decide from the evidence they heard whether Leslie's judgment was impaired enough to convict her of first-degree murder or if it should be manslaughter.

In 1978, a second trial took place. The prosecution added charges of theft of clothing, food, and money, all of which had been taken from the house. The additional charges made it a felony murder, which undermined the idea of Leslie being of diminished capacity. Leslie and her cohorts were committing felonies, and the thefts and murders happened in the commission of those felonies.

Leslie was out on bond during the second trial, which lasted about six months. The jury returned a guilty verdict, and later she was sentenced to life in prison with the possibility of parole. A year later, Leslie claimed that she was high almost the whole trial because she was getting LSD in prison.

Leslie van Houten was finally released on parole on July 11, 2023, after serving fifty-two years. She was sent to the transitional living facility, where she will be supervised for up to three years. Her first scheduled leave was in 2024. Leslie had been rejected for parole a total of 23 times.

Linda Kasabian

Linda Kasabian grew up in Milford, New Hampshire, but her father moved out while she was still very young to remarry another woman. Her mother also remarried Jake Byrd, who, according to Linda, was abusive to her and her mother. By the time Linda was sixteen, she decided to marry Robert Peasley, but the marriage lasted only a few months before they got divorced. Linda then headed to Miami, where her father had been living with his new wife. Things didn't work out very well for them, as his new wife didn't want Linda around her house.

Linda then met Robert Kasabian, and they were married on September 20, 1967. They had met while both were living in a hippie commune in the Boston area. Early in 1968, the couple had a daughter named Tanya. Linda and Robert began arguing, and Linda took her daughter and moved back home with her mother. Later that same year, Robert called Linda at her mother's house and asked her to return to California to try to reconcile. She agreed and moved in with him in Topanga Canyon.

Robert and Linda began to fight regularly, just as they had when they were living together before. Feeling rejected, Linda decided to take her daughter, Tanya, and stay with a girlfriend of hers, Gypsy, who had been living in a hippie commune on a ranch. This move would ultimately lead to her joining the Manson Family, living on Spahn Ranch, led by Charlie Manson.

Now part of the Family, on the night of August 8, 1969, Linda headed into town with Tex Watson, Susan Atkins, and Patricia Krenwinkel to what she believed would be another "creepy-crawley." A creepy-crawley was where they would break into someone's home, rearrange items, consume some of their food, and cause damage. They weren't out to hurt anybody, but they thought it funny to freak people out who would later return home, and things were all moved around.

Watson told her where to drive. She was the driver because she was the only one who had a driver's license. Once they arrived at 10050 Cielo Drive, Linda was told to wait outside. The other three got out of the car and began making plans.

Just then, a car started to drive away from the house and towards them. Tex suddenly got enraged and ran out in front of the vehicle to stop it. The car stopped, and Tex went over to the car window, pulled a gun out of his pants, and shot the driver four times.

The following night, the LaBianca murders happened. Shortly after that, Linda became terrified. She took one of the cars and drove away. She left the commune and went into hiding. She was unable to bring her daughter, Tanya, with her at the time.

Weeks later, when Manson and some of the Family were arrested and charged with murder, Linda claimed possession of her daughter. She agreed to testify against Manson and some of the others for immunity. During the trial, when Linda was testifying, Manson or the Family members would repeatedly disrupt her testimony. One time, Manson ran his finger across his throat as if to say, "This is what is going to happen to you if you keep talking." Susan Atkins would whisper the words, "You're Killing Us."

Linda gave birth to a baby boy on March 10, 1970. The father was missing at that time, and Tanya was in an undisclosed location.

Patricia Krenwinkel

Patricia Krenwinkel was born on December 3, 1947, in Los Angeles, where she lived with her father, who was an insurance salesman, her stay-at-home mother, and stepsister Charlene.

Krenwinkel always struggled with her weight, and because she had an endocrine issue, she had an excessive amount of hair on her face. She would often be teased and laughed at by her classmates during school, and never really formed a group of friends.

Charlene got Patricia some diet pills, which back then consisted mainly of high amounts of caffeine, and when she lost some weight, she still didn't like her looks at all. Patricia then started to look for boys that she could have sex with to help fill her insecurities.

At the age of seventeen, in 1964, her parents divorced. Patricia stayed in Los Angeles with her father until she graduated from high school. She then moved to Alabama to attend a Catholic college there, but dropped out at the end of the first semester and returned to California.

Patricia returned to Los Angeles and moved in with her stepsister, Charlene, who had an apartment on Manhattan Beach. She got a job as a clerk. At the time, Charlene was using heroin regularly and starting to become addicted.

In the Fall of 1967, Patricia came home after work to find that Charlene was having a party in their apartment. Charles Manson was there. He had approached her and began to talk to her in his "Charlie way," making her feel that she was everything to him. They would spend the night together. During their romance, he would constantly tell her how beautiful she was, which would often bring tears to her eyes. As a result, she would become one of his most devoted followers.

Patricia Krenwinkel became Charlie's third follower to join him after Mary Brunner and Lynette Fromme. The four-member Family decided to go to

Seattle. Manson didn't like the vibes of the city, so he took the girls and moved to San Francisco.

Soon, the Family grew, and Charlie found an old school bus that they painted and decorated to look very psychedelic. They toured around the country for a year and a half before settling back in Los Angeles. Patricia Krenwinkel would later say that these were the best times for them, as all they did was have fun by running through the trees and putting flowers in their hair. It was as if they had no cares in the world.

After they returned to Los Angeles, Charlie had the girls go out to look for celebrities or rock stars for him, as he was trying to make a connection to have his music heard and secure a record contract. One of the things he had them do was to go out on Sunset Drive and hitchhike around so that they could meet people.

During the Summer of 1968, Krenwinkel was out hitchhiking with Ella Bailey, another member of the Family. A handsome man drove up and asked them if they would like to go back to his house and have some raw milk and cookies. They both said yes and then jumped in his car.

The man ended up being the drummer for the rock band, the Beach Boys, Dennis Wilson. All of them returned to his place and had milk and cookies.

Dennis was serious about that, and he did give them raw milk, as that was the only kind of milk he would drink. Later in the afternoon, Wilson had to go to his recording studio to work on some music with his band, so the girls left.

When Krenwinkel and Bailey returned to see Charlie, he told them who they had been picked up by. Charlie got excited and loaded several of the girls into the car, telling them to lead the way to Wilson's house. The girls had never heard of the Beach Boys before, but Manson was familiar with them.

Later that night, around midnight, Wilson returned to his home to find the Manson Family had moved into his house. When he walked into the house, many of the girls were naked or only wearing their underwear, eating his food, drinking his liquor, and playing Beatles albums on his record player.

The Family ended up staying at Wilson's house for several months before Dennis told them that they had to leave because he was giving up the house and going on tour for a while. Manson and his followers would move to Spahn Ranch, located in the hills of the San Fernando Valley.

On the night of August 8th, Krenwinkel accompanied Tex Watson, Susan Atkins, and Linda Kasabian to the house on Cielo Drive, which was owned by Sharon Tate and her husband, Roman Polanski. She participated in the killings that went on there more than the other two women did.

After they entered the Tate house, Frykowski was woken up shortly after midnight by Charles Tex Watson. When he asked him what time it was, Tex proceeded to kick him in the head. Frykowski got up off the floor and asked him who he was. Tex said, "I'm the devil, and I'm here to do the devil's business."

While this was going on, the Manson girls searched the house to find everyone and bring them all back to the living room.

Krenwinkel entered Abigail Folger's bedroom, where she had been lying on her bed reading. Krenwinkel told her to get out of bed and follow her out into the living room. Folger thought that Krenwinkel was a high partygoer who was at the house looking for someone else, so she told her no.

Krenwinkel got mad and walked over to Folger on the bed, grabbed her by the hair, and pulled her off. Folger started to get up and began to fight back when Krenwinkel pulled her knife out and swiped it at Folger's face. Folger dropped to the floor, and Krenwinkel grabbed Folger's left leg near her foot and dragged her out into the living room without any struggle.

Once they got there and Krenwinkel let go of her leg, Folger got up and began to fight with her. The two wrestled and fell to the ground. Krenwinkel was starting to lose control, so she began to stab Folger. Once she believed that Folger was dead, she got back up, only to have Folger run out of the room and out into the back lawn. Krenwinkel chased her and tackled her. Once they both fell again, she started to stab her some more. Krenwinkel began to weaken and could no longer control Folger, so she yelled for Tex, who ran outside behind them. He ended up killing Folger.

The following night, Krenwinkel joined Manson, Tex Watson, and Leslie Van Houten at the home of Leno and Rosemary LaBianca on Waverly Drive. During the events of this night, Krenwinkel felt empowered because of the prior evening's killings. This time, she did not need to be ordered to do the killing. In fact, she stabbed Rosemary LaBianca with vigor. She also got excited to be able to write on the walls with the blood from their victims. She appeared to have fun getting the blood as well. Krenwinkel even left a carving fork in Leno LaBianca's stomach after carving the word "War" across his chest.

When the police raided Spahn Ranch on August 16th, they were looking for stolen vehicles. Three days later, the charges were dropped because the search warrant had the wrong date written in it.

Manson relocated to Barker Ranch, which was situated farther out in the desert of Death Valley. He thought that it would be better to move out there to get away from the police, and it would help to isolate his Family from outside influences.

While out in Death Valley, the Family spent most of their time stealing vehicles and converting them for desert use or stealing dune buggies. Everyone was preparing for the upcoming race war between the Blacks and Whites. As Manson had told them about a hidden place in the desert that they needed to find to be safe from the Blacks, many members would spend their day out searching for it.

October 10th came, and in the early morning, police raided the Manson Family yet again, also looking for stolen vehicles. Krenwinkel's father came and bailed her out of jail. He sent her to stay with her aunt, who lived in Mobile, Alabama.

Over the next month, Susan Atkins, who remained in jail, began to tell police about the Tate and LaBianca murders. Warrants for the arrest for murder were issued on many of Manson's followers, including

Krenwinkel. Police found her at her aunts on December 1, 1969, and the following day she was indicted for seven counts of murder in the first degree.

For the next two months, Krenwinkel fought extradition to Los Angeles, claiming that Manson would kill her, and that was the reason she moved to Alabama in the first place.

In February the following year, Krenwinkel was finally sent to Los Angeles to stand trial along with Manson, Van Houten, and Susan Atkins. Tex Watson wasn't located and extradited until much later, so he stood trial on his own.

During the trial, Krenwinkel appeared to show little interest in anyone being questioned on the stand or in what the attorneys were telling the jury. Instead, she was focused on drawing pictures or doodling the whole time, seldom looking up. All three female Manson defendants, Krenwinkel, Atkins, and Van Houten, followed Manson's instructions well. They walked to the court together, holding hands and singing songs. Once, they even shaved their heads bald. Another time, they painted an "X" on their foreheads. All of these acts were intended to demonstrate the Family's unity.

After their nine-month trial was over, Krenwinkel was convicted on all seven charges of murder: the August 9th Cielo Drive killings of Abigail Folger,

Steven Parent, Sharon Tate, Jay Sebring, and Wojciech Frykowski, and for the August 10th killings of Leno and Rosemary LaBianca.

Krenwinkel was sentenced to death on March 29, 1971. But like the other Manson Family members who were convicted of murder, her sentence was later commuted to life in prison due to the Supreme Court decision in 1972.

Krenwinkel's first parole hearing was in July 1978. It was denied. There were another fourteen parole hearings for Krenwinkel, and she was rejected in all of them. At the last parole hearing, her attorney claimed that she was dealing with battered woman syndrome, which Manson had inflicted. She claimed that he often beat her during the time of the murders. A year later, the parole board declined her application.

On her fifteenth attempt, on May 26, 2022, Krenwinkel was granted parole. However, on October 14, 2022, California Governor Gavin Newsom reversed that decision. Patricia Krenwinkel remains in prison today.

On May 21, 2025, Krenwinkel was again approved for parole. However, at the time of this writing, she hasn't yet been released. The Governor has yet to decide whether to reverse that decision.

When Krenwinkel was initially sent to prison, she remained close to Susan Atkins and Leslie Van Houten. The three of them followed Manson completely without question. After serving a couple of years, Krenwinkel started to become weary of Manson and began to distance herself from the other girls.

Over time, Krenwinkel joined Alcoholics Anonymous and Narcotics Anonymous and began studying correspondence courses through the University of La Verne, earning her bachelor's degree in human services. Her degree led her to teach other illiterate prisoners how to read. She has also become very social, participating in sports and attending dances in prison.

Susan Atkins

Susan Denise Atkins was born in San Gabriel, California, on May 8, 1948, and lived with her parents, Edward and Jeanne Atkins, and two siblings in San Jose, California. She was known as a quiet, self-conscious girl at school who belonged to both the school's glee club and the family's church choir. Her mother died in 1961, when Susan was only thirteen years old, and her father moved them to Los Banos, California.

A few months after that, Edward got a job working on the new San Luis Dam construction project and needed to move there, so he left Susan behind to take care of her younger brother, Steven. Relatives were also helping to take care of Susan and her brother, but Susan had to get a job as well to help support them financially.

In 1966, when the Christmas school break began, she ran away to San Francisco with two friends she had attended school with. Early in 1967, Susan took a job as a stripper in Los Angeles and became immensely popular. Even the leader of the Church of Satan, Anton LaVey, hired her for a performance.

Later in 1967, Susan attended a house party, where a man named Charlie Manson was playing guitar for the crowd. They met at this party and struck up a friendship. A couple of weeks later, the house where Susan was renting was raided by police, and she had to find a new place to live. Charlie invited her to come with him and his Family, who had a bus and were going to take a trip across America.

Susan accompanied the Family on their trip, and Manson dubbed her "Sadie Mae Glutz." She even had a false identification made for her under that same name. During the Family bus trip, Susan started to believe that Manson was the second coming of Jesus. Soon afterwards, Manson and his Family moved to live on the Spahn Ranch, located in Southern California's San Fernando Valley.

On October 7, 1968, Susan gave birth to a son, whose father was Bruce White, a member of the

Family. The son was named Zezozose Zadfrack Glutz by Manson.

When the Summer of 1969 came, Manson was desperate to get enough money and dune buggies to move his followers out to Barker Ranch in the Death Valley Desert. Police were also becoming suspicious of the Manson Family because they were hearing rumors about them being behind some of the car thefts.

Manson was also encouraging his members to sell drugs to make some money as well. One of their suppliers was a man named Gary Hinman, who made mescaline in the basement of his home. During some of the visits by different Family members to Hinman's home, they heard that he had inherited a substantial amount of money. At first, Manson tried to convince him to come out and join his commune, but Hinman wasn't interested. He liked living alone.

One of Manson Family regulars, Bobby Beausoleil, wasn't officially part of the commune. Still, he partied at the ranch a lot and would often arrange drug sales to different bikers who partied at Spahn Ranch with the Family. He got the drugs from Hinman.

On one of the sales he made to the Straight Satan biker gang at Spahn Ranch, he took their money and went to Hinman's house and exchanged it for the drugs. Then he returned and gave it to the bikers. Beausoleil often did this for a cut of the money and some drugs. But with this sale he made in July, the bikers came back to him and told him the drugs were bad, so he would have to get their money back for them.

When he told Charlie what was going on, Manson told him to bring Susan Atkins and Mary Brunner with him when he went out to Hinman's house. After they arrived at the house, Beausoleil told him that they wanted the drug money back, but Hinman said that he didn't have it anymore. So Beausoleil beat him up.

They called Manson and told him what was going on. Manson, along with Bruce Davis, showed up at Hinman's a few hours later. When Hinman opened the door, Manson took his sword and sliced Hinman's ear off. He then threatened Hinman. Before he left, he told Beausoleil, "You know what to do."

After more beating and torture, all Beausoleil managed to do was to get Hinman to sign the titles to his two cars over to him. Neither vehicle was worth very much, perhaps totaling around $2,000 combined.

Beausoleil had left the room, leaving Susan Atkins alone with Hinman, who got up and began to fight with her, so she started to stab him. Atkins wasn't able to control Hinman, so she screamed out for Beausoleil. When he came back into the room, he tackled Hinman and began to stab him as well. Beausoleil would eventually stab him to death.

Then they wrote "Political Piggie" on the wall with Hinman's blood. They also left what appeared to be a panther paw print on the wall. The print mark was to try to make it look like the murder was committed by the Black Panther group.

Later that summer, on August 7th, Beausoleil was found asleep in the back of one of Hinman's cars. He was still wearing the same clothes that he had worn when he stabbed Hinman to death, and he was still all covered in blood. Police searched the car and found the knife that was used to murder Hinman in the tire well. He was taken in and arrested for the murder.

The day after Beausoleil's arrest, August 8th, Manson decided that to get Beausoleil free, they would do a copycat style murder. They would do the murders in much the same way and leave a bloody panther paw behind. This time, Manson wanted to murder people who were either rich or celebrities so that the murders would make a big splash with the press.

Manson had Tex Watson take the lead and bring Susan Atkins, Linda Kasabian, and Patricia Krenwinkel with him. Manson told the girls firmly that they were to do anything Tex told them to do, without question.

After the murders, they returned to Spahn Ranch and told Charlie what happened. Manson was upset and didn't trust that they left things the way they should have. He got into the car and drove them all back to Cielo Drive, making sure everything was in order.

The next day, after the news broke, and Manson wasn't hearing what he thought he would from the press, that there were murders of some rich celebrity-type people by the Black Panthers, he knew that he had to strike again.

That evening, he would go himself, and this time he brought Tex Watson, Susan Atkins, Patricia Krenwinkel, Linda Kasabian, Leslie Van Houten, and Steve Grogan with him. He took them to the La Biancas' home, located on Waverly Drive. He entered the house with Tex and approached Leno LaBianca. Tex tied him up.

Once he explained to Tex what he wanted done and how the place needed to be left, he went back to the car and sent Krenwinkel and Van Houten into the house before leaving with the others.

On August 16th, less than a week after the LaBianca murders, police raided the Spahn Ranch looking for stolen cars. They found some of the stolen vehicles they were looking for, but because of an error in the date on the search warrant, all charges were dropped three days later.

Manson moved most of his followers to Barker Ranch in Death Valley to escape outside influences and distance himself from the police. They resumed stealing more vehicles, just as they had before. Eventually, police caught up with them again, and in October 1969, police raided Manson and his followers again at his new location, Barker Ranch.

While Atkins was in jail for car theft, she met up with two of her friends from before, Virginia Graham and Ronnie Howard. Over the following weeks, she would tell them about the murders that she and the Family were part of and many of the other illegal activities they did. One key highlight that Atkins bragged about was how she responded to Sharon Tate when she pleaded for her unborn baby's life. "Look bitch, I don't care about you. I don't care about your baby. You're going to die, and I don't feel a thing about it."

As with many murder cases that happen, we are left with the killers to tell us who did what. Atkins initially said that she stabbed Tate, but later said that she was lying and that it was Tex Watson who stabbed her. Later, Tex would take responsibility for Tate's murder. Is he just protecting Atkins? Was he trying to look big by saying that he murdered Tate? We know that Atkins couldn't help but brag about anything she did to anyone who might listen.

Both Graham and Howard were so sickened from the stories that Atkins had told them, they both went to the prison authorities and told them. The auto theft charges were soon elevated to murder. Eventually, both Graham and Howard would get the $25,000 reward that Tate's husband, Roman Polanski, offered for information leading to the conviction of her murderers.

Initially, the detectives offered Atkins a plea deal for her giving evidence and testimony to convict Charles Manson. They would, in turn, give her complete immunity. When Vincent Bugliosi took over the case, he immediately said, "No! We don't need to give that gal anything at all! We will do it without her. She needs to pay for her involvement!"

Later, Bugliosi would alter his plan slightly. Instead of complete immunity, he would take the death penalty off the table and only go for a life imprisonment penalty against Atkins in turn for her testimony. After Atkins was convicted of first-degree murder and the jury went into deliberation for the penalty phase of the crime, they returned with a death sentence for Atkins. They refused to go along with Bugliosi based on Atkins' testimony because she seemed to take pleasure in her descriptions of murdering the victims. The jury could do this legally because Atkins had filed a statement claiming that what she had said to Bugliosi was not true. As a result, it also meant that Atkins did not cooperate with the prosecution, and her immunity 'no death penalty' deal was therefore void.

Later, Atkins would say that she backed away from the agreement only because Manson had told her, through messages, that it would be "better for her son" if she didn't testify against any of the Family members.

As Atkins told the jury about holding Tate down when Tex was stabbing her, Atkins seemed to want the jury to say to her what a great job she did, even though Tate put up such an aggressive struggle. She was able to keep her under control so that Tex could "get the job done."

Atkins also described when Tate pleaded for her unborn baby's life, and she replied, "Woman, I have no mercy for you!" Even though it had been softened for the jury, they still found it too horrific.

Atkins claimed that the words she spoke to Tate were not directed at her but rather meant for herself and to help reassure her that she was doing the right thing. Atkins later tried to change her story by claiming she lied to both Howard and Graham when she said that she had tasted Tate's blood.

Atkins was also tried and convicted for the Gary Hinman murder, where she pleaded guilty and testified that she was there, but she had no idea that they were going to kill Hinman. She believed that they were there only to get money. Later in Atkins' book, she said something different. She said she knew what they were going to do, and she took some part in the murder as well.

As with the other Manson girls, she was sent to the newly built death row for women on April 23, 1970. Atkins' sentence was also commuted to life imprisonment after the California Supreme Court decision of 1972, which in effect invalidated all previous death sentences given in California before 1972.

In 1974, while Atkins was in her cell, she claimed that her cell door opened, and out of nowhere, a bright light came over her. She believed that it was the light of Jesus, and he told her that God had forgiven her for all of her sins. Atkins would write about these experiences in a book published in 1977, *titled Child of Satan, Child of God.*

After this, she became a model prisoner and participated in several prison programs, even receiving two commendations for her assistance to guards. Atkins was also married twice during her incarceration. One of her marriages, which only lasted a few months, was to Donald Lee Laisure on September 2, 1981. They originally met through letters sent by mail. Laisure was a famed conman, and Atkins was his thirty-sixth wife. He divorced Atkins so that he could marry his thirty-seventh wife.

In the Summer of 1987, Atkins got married again to a Harvard Law School graduate, James W. Whitehouse, who would also be her legal counsel during her parole hearing until she died. At the time of their marriage, Atkins was thirty-eight and Whitehouse was fifteen years younger at twenty-four.

Laisure filed a lawsuit against the Federal Court, believing that Atkins was a political prisoner and this was why she had always been denied parole. These proceedings resulted in a three-year ban from Atkins, preventing her from reapplying for parole.

On June 1, 2005, Atkins was given a special parole hearing based on compassion as she was now ill with brain cancer and was given only six months left to live. She was denied again.

In April 2008, Atkins was permanently hospitalized, and her left leg had to be amputated. The operation ultimately cost taxpayers over $1.15 million for medical expenses and over $300,000 for the cost of full-time guards to protect her in the hospital.

Atkins died while in prison at the Central California Women's Facility in Chowchilla, California, on September 24, 2009. She had lost her parental rights to her son after she was convicted of murder. At that time, none of her relatives would take the boy, so the court changed his name and placed him for adoption. Susan never saw him again.

Ruth Ann Moorehouse

Protestant Minister Dean Allen Moorehouse, who was living in Toronto, Canada, with Audrey Sirpless, had Ruth Ann on January 6, 1953. When they were living in Minnesota previously, they had three other children: two girls and a boy. Soon after Rutn Ann was born, the family moved to Campbell, California, where she attended Westmont High School.

In the Spring of 1967, when Dean Moorehouse was driving home from work, he picked up a hitchhiker, who ended up being Charles Manson. The two men got along well, and Moorehouse invited Manson over to his house, now in San Jose, for dinner.

That night, the two of them sang religious tunes, with Charlie playing the piano, and they discussed scripture. Manson spent the night, and the next morning, Moorehouse told Manson that he was always welcome in his house.

Manson began visiting the Moorehouse home a couple of times a week. During one of his visits, the only person home was Ruth Ann, who was fourteen at the time. He invited her to accompany him on a trip to the coast. Manson had gotten a Volkswagen Microbus on an earlier visit from one of the neighbors in exchange for a piano, which had belonged to Dean Moorehouse.

When Dean and Audrey returned home later that day and found out what had happened, they called the police to report their daughter as a runaway. A few days after that, on June 28, 1967, police found them at the beach. Manson was arrested for trying to interfere with the police, and Ruth Ann was brought back home.

Right after this, trouble began between Dean and Audrey. They started fighting over Dean's friendship with Manson. She thought he was weird and a bad influence on their daughter, Ruth Ann. She began to worry about her other children. Eventually, Audrey decided she would leave and move in with her sister.

The following Spring, on May 20, 1968, Ruth Ann married Edward Heuvel Horst, a twenty-three-year-old bus driver in Santa Cruz. Ruth Ann wanted to escape her father, and at fifteen, this was the only way she could think of to do it. Manson had given her this idea so that she could come and live with him. The day after she was married, she left for Los Angeles and the Manson Family.

When Dean heard about Ruth Ann leaving her husband after just one day and moving to Los Angeles, he figured it was best to go down there and see what was going on with her. He soon learned that Manson and the girls were all living with Beach Boy drummer Dennis Wilson at his house on Sunset Drive, so he went there looking for his daughter.

Dean parked his car on the road in front of Wilson's house and walked to the front door, and rang the doorbell. Manson joyously answered the door and was thrilled to see Dean. He bent down on his knees and began to kiss Dean's toes. Once Dean entered the house, Manson gave him a hit of LSD. He stayed there all summer, trading a room in Wilson's guesthouse for landscaping the property. When Manson left the Wilson estate and took his Family to Spahn Ranch, Dean followed them there as he was slowly becoming a devout Manson follower. Yet Dean ended up leaving the Family within a year.

When Manson met Terry Melcher, he had some of his girls with him, including Ruth Ann. Melcher liked her, and the two began to have a sexual relationship. Soon after that, Melcher offered her a job at his home, which at that time was the Cielo Drive house, which would later be the scene of the Tate murders. When Ruth Ann showed up to start her first day of work there, Melcher's live-in girlfriend at the time, Candice Bergen, told her to leave and never come back again.

Ruth Ann became a valuable Family member to Manson, not only for her ability to earn a substantial income through panhandling or stealing food, but also because she was skilled with children. She would ultimately become the Family's full-time caretaker for the kids.

When the police first raided Manson and his Family, it was at Spahn Ranch on August 16, 1969. They were looking for stolen vehicles, and Ruth Ann was one of the followers they arrested. The police wrote the search warrant with he wrong date on it, so all charges were dropped, and everyone was released three days later.

Ruth Ann was one of the followers that Manson sent to go live at Barker Ranch out in the desert, because all the children went there too. While she was living there, Susan Atkins told her the story about the murders that she was involved in at Cielo Drive. It was said that Ruth Ann was excited about what they had done and wanted to get involved. She just couldn't wait to make her first kill.

When the police did their second raid, this time at the Barker Ranch, Ruth Ann, along with twelve others, including Manson, were arrested. She was released after a couple of weeks and decided to move in with her mother, who was now remarried and living in Minnesota. Out of sight, out of mind, at least that's how it was for Ruth Ann, who stopped hearing from any of the Manson Family for about six months.

Then, out of the blue one day, Squeaky began to contact her. Of course, this wasn't just Squeaky all of a sudden remembering how much she loved Ruth Ann and felt it was time to call her. No, instead, it was the beginning of the Tate and LaBianca murder trials against Charlie and some of the other girls. Squeaky needed to rally the troops, garner as much support as possible for Charlie, and at the same time ensure that the prosecution hadn't turned any of the former Family members.

Eventually, Squeaky talked Ruth Ann into returning to Los Angeles, where she would become part of the regular support squad of Manson girls with an X on their foreheads, standing outside the courthouse and chanting about love. Ruth Ann was slowly being pulled back into a loyal following of Manson again.

Once Squeaky had learned that Bugliosi was getting ex-Family member Barbara Hoyt to testify against Charlie in the Fall of 1970, she planned to stop that from happening. At first, Squeaky thought that she could meet with Hoyt and talk her out of it. But after several phone calls and still being unable to convince Hoyt not to testify, she offered her a free trip to Hawaii.

When Hoyt heard this, she was excited. She had never been there before, so she agreed. Squeaky arranged for Hoyt and Ruth Ann to obtain free plane tickets, as well as credit cards under the aliases of Amy Riley and Jill Morgan. Soon, the two of them were off to Hawaii for a fun time.

The first couple of days went well for them. They stayed at a beautiful hotel, had the opportunity to order all the food and drinks they wanted, walked on the beach, and went shopping. It was wonderful.

On day three, September 9th, Ruth Ann came up to Hoyt and told her that she had to leave and return to Los Angeles that day. Hoyt could stay in Hawaii as long as she wanted, and it would still be all free for her.

They took a cab to the airport, and while they were waiting, they each ordered something to eat. When the food came up, Hoyt paid for it while Ruth Ann took it outside. When Hoyt got outside, Ruth Ann gave her the hamburger that she ordered, and she ate it. The boarding announcement came over the loudspeaker, so Ruth Ann stood up. Before she left to catch the plane, she said, "Could you imagine what it would be like if there were ten tabs of acid in that burger?" She laughed and quickly ran away.

Hoyt got a cab back to the hotel where she had been staying, but when she got out of the cab, she started to feel strange. Hoyt had felt this feeling before when she had been high on acid. Then she realized that Ruth Ann had drugged her. She ran into the lobby bathroom and began to put her fingers down her throat to make herself throw up.

Hoyt seemed to calm down a bit and decided she would go outside for some fresh air. As she slowly walked, the dizziness returned, this time with even greater intensity. So, she walked into the first building she saw, which happened to be the Salvation Army.

A man there asked her if there was anything that he could do for her, as she didn't look very well. Hoyt told the man to call Mr. Bugliosi and then passed out. An ambulance was called, and she was taken to the hospital.

She was now ready to testify against Charlie, who tried to have her killed.

On December 18, 1970, when police made arrests for the attempted murder of Barbara Hoyt, Ruth Ann Moorehouse was one of them. She also had to take the stand on the Tate and LaBianca murder cases in February 1971, and at this time, she was around eight months pregnant.

A month later, Ruth Ann pleaded no contest to conspiracy to dissuade a witness, Barbara Hoyt, and the attempted murder charges were dropped. She was sentenced to serve ninety days in jail, but she failed to appear at the hearing. Instead, she had run away and gone to live with her sister in Carson City, Nevada, where she gave birth to her daughter on April 10, 1971.

Ruth Ann moved to Reno after meeting and marrying Harold Fowler, a construction worker, and they had a daughter together in 1973. Two years later, the FBI found her. She was arrested for fleeing her jail sentence and was now charged again with the attempted murder of Barbara Hoyt. Her lawyer argued that she only ran before because she was nine months pregnant and didn't want to have to give birth to her baby in prison. In November, the judge set her free because of the hard life she had lived.

After her release, Ruth Ann moved back to Minnesota and married for a third time, Dale Warren Geist. The couple had a daughter who only lived until 1981. She was only seven years old at the time. The couple ended their marriage in divorce. She also had plastic surgery to have the scar of the swastika on her forehead removed.

Sandra Good

Sandra Good was born on February 20, 1944, in San Diego, California. After she finished high school, Sandra spent seven years in various colleges, including California State University in Sacramento, San Francisco State College, and the University of Oregon. Still, she would never complete a degree in any of her studies.

While attending San Francisco State College, she met Joel Pugh, a lab technician. The two began dating and became extremely close in a short time.

In the Spring of 1968, Good met Manson at a party, and his spiritual beliefs captivated her. Before long, she began following Manson everywhere that he went. But Joel didn't like that, nor did he like Manson, whom he thought was a fraud.

In the Summer, when Manson and his Family moved to Spahn Ranch, Good joined them, leaving Joel behind. Manson didn't like Joel either, and he began to tell Good that Joel was an evil man and she should stay away from him. Manson had his eye on the $2,000 trust fund that Good was living off for his use.

Joel became unhappy with losing Good. He quit his job at the university, gave up his apartment, and moved back to Minnesota to live with his parents. One day, out of the blue, Good appeared at Joel's parents' home to see him. Good was pregnant, and she wanted to use Joel's last name for the baby. He didn't like that and told her no.

Good had the baby on September 16th, naming him Ivan Pugh. She used Joel's last name for the baby's birth certificate soon after Joel left the country to travel around the world. Later, it was determined that Ivan's father was Bobby Beausoleil, who was convicted of murdering Gary Hinman.

The week before the Cielo Drive murders happened, Charlie had sent Good and Mary Brunner out to get some clothes and supplies. They were arrested for using stolen credit cards to make purchases and were subsequently taken into custody and then transported to jail.

Good was released on August 12th and went back to the ranch. Both the Tate and LaBianca murders had already happened, but she wasn't aware of who committed them or that any of the Family was involved. Four days later, the police conducted a raid on Spahn Ranch, searching for stolen cars, and Good was one of the followers arrested that day. She was released in three days, as all charges against her had been dismissed. The police had dated the search warrant incorrectly, making it invalid. Therefore, anything they found in the search couldn't be used in court.

On December 1, 1969, Joel Pugh's dead body was found in London, England, in the Hotel Talgart. Both of his wrists and throat had been sliced with a knife. Police took note of writing on his bedroom mirror, but there was nothing mentioned about committing suicide. Detectives would rule his death a drug-induced suicide.

Bugliosi heard about the death of Joel Pugh and became suspicious about his death because one of Manson's crew, Bruce Davis, who was also a Scientologist, was there working for the church at the same time Pugh was found dead. Bugliosi kept a close eye on Davis, but no charges were ever filed against him.

After the trials of the Manson Family members were completed, several of his followers who were on the outside remained faithfully devoted to Manson. They continued to do everything they could to try to get him free by causing trouble wherever they could. Squeaky Fromme was standing in the public area of the California State Capitol grounds while President Gerald Ford, who was on his way to see the Governor on September 5, 1975. As Ford walked by, Squeaky raised her arm, and in her hand was an M1911 gun. She pointed it directly at his head and pulled the trigger, but she didn't chamber the round, so it never fired.

Just after Squeaky was arrested, Good was interviewed on the A.M. radio station *WWL* in New Orleans, where she told the interviewer that the Ford assassination attempt was just the first of many more to come. Good now claimed that she was part of a group called the International People's Court of Retrobution. She would go on to name different business executives whom she accused of polluting the country. Good would threaten the lives of these executives and their families on air that day.

By December 1975, Good, along with another Family member, Susan Murphy, was arrested and charged with conspiracy to send threatening letters through the mail in Sacramento, California. The pair had collectively threatened the lives of more than one hundred and seventy people. After only three months of trial, they were both found guilty, and Good received a fifteen-year prison sentence on April 13, 1976.

She served a ten-year term of her sentence in West Virginia at the Federal Correctional Institution for Women. One of the conditions of her parole was that she couldn't live in California, so she moved to Vermont and changed her name to Sandra Collins. She remained under this alias until 1999, when someone discovered her true identity.

After Good completed her parole, she moved back to California in Hanford, because it was close to where Manson was in prison, even though she wouldn't ever be allowed to visit him as she was a convicted felon. Good then started *Access Manson*, a website promoting Charlie, which made her feel good because she was doing something to help him out. Even during her last public interview in 2019, Good was still worshipping Charlie and everything he had done.

Lynette "Squeaky " Fromme

Lynette Fromme was born in Santa Monica on October 22, 1948. Her father was an aeronautical engineer, William Millar Fromme. Her mother, Helen, took the time to train Lynette in dance, and she became part of the Westchester Lariats, which toured both the United States and Europe. They ended up becoming famous enough to play the White House and appear on the popular *Lawrence Welk Television Show*.

When Lynette turned fifteen in 1963, her family moved to Redondo Beach. After entering high school there, she started to experiment with drugs and drinking alcohol, and soon she began skipping school, and her grades went down fast. She graduated in 1966 and moved away from home, staying with some of her friends.

Lynette's father had her move home and attend college, a decision that lasted only about two months. He kicked her out of the house because she was constantly screaming and swearing at her parents and refused to do anything they asked her to do. Lynette dropped out of college and moved to Venice Beach, where she would spend her nights.

Often during the day, she sat on road curbs or at bus stops to pass the time. One day, Charles Manson got off the bus and he noticed her sitting alone and walked up to her and asked, "Your parents threw you out, didn't they?" He then turned around and began walking away from her. Lynette grabbed her bags and followed him. This chance encounter was in 1967, just after he was released from Terminal Island Prison. Lynette would become his second long-term follower.

Manson was living with Mary Brunner in her apartment at the time, and when Manson brought Lynette back to their apartment, Mary was at work. The two ended up having sex, and when Mary returned home, she was angry at Charlie. Eventually, he persuaded Mary to let Lynette live with them. When the Manson Family moved to Spahn Ranch, the owner, George Spahn, gave

Lynette the nickname "Squeaky," which stuck from then on.

After the arrests of Manson and his followers in 1969, those involved with the Tate–LaBianca murders, Squeaky remained one of Charlie's leading outside actors. She constantly received messages from him while he was in jail and passed them on to the intended recipient. She was also the one who would locate Family members who had left and moved away, ensuring they weren't involved in the trial and would not cause any further problems for Charlie. Squeaky was also one of Manson's followers who would camp outside of the courthouse with her head shaved and an X marked onto her forehead. She preached to anyone who walked by and stopped to listen.

Squeaky was never involved in any of the murders, and so she was never arrested ot charged for them. Later, she was accused of attempting to prevent witnesses from testifying in court, and when she was subpoenaed to testify, she refused to do so. As a result, the judge charged her with contempt of court. On both occasions, she would only receive sentences of less than a year in prison.

After the trials of Manson were over in 1973, Squeaky began to write a book on the Manson Family, which also included some of her photos and drawings about the murders that happened, which were quite incriminating, so she decided that she wasn't going to have it published. This book was later published in 2018 under the title *Reflexion*.

In the early morning of September 5, 1975, Squeaky went to the Capitol Building in Sacramento because she heard that President Gerald Ford was going to be there to visit Governor Jerry Brown. As Ford walked by, Squeaky, who was standing among the crowd of people on the grounds, pulled out her Colt M1911 .45 caliber semi-automatic pistol and aimed it at his head. Standing only a couple of feet away, she pulled the trigger. But nothing happened. Though she had four bullets loaded in the magazine, there were no rounds in the chamber, so the gun didn't fire. The Secret Service immediately grabbed her and threw her to the ground.

Squeaky was arrested, tried, and convicted of attempting to assassinate the president, and she was sentenced to a life term in prison. While in prison, she was constantly in fights with other inmates.

On December 28, 1987, Squeaky escaped from prison to meet Manson but was captured two days later.

Squeaky became eligible for parole in 2005, at which time she waived her right to a hearing. She was eventually approved for parole in 2008, but remained in prison because she had to serve out her sentence for her attempt to escape back in 1987.

Squeaky was finally released from prison on August 14, 2009, and she moved to Mercy, New York, with her boyfriend, Robert Valdner.

References

1. The Times | UK News, World News and Opinion
2. "Manson Family Members and Associates" *Helter Skelter* 0-553-14683-1
3. *"Ex-Manson follower Susan Atkins dies"*. *www.cnn.com*
4. Fox, Margalit (September 26, 2009). "Susan Atkins, Manson Follower, Dies at 61". *The New York Times*.
5. *Child of Satan, Child of God: Her Own Story, Susan Atkins*. Menelorelin Dorenay's Publishing. ISBN 978-0-9831364-8-4.
6. Transcript of Atkins's 2005 parole hearing.
7. Johnston, Lori (July 27, 2019). *"Gary Hinman: The Forgotten Manson Family Victim"*. *Medium. New York City: A Medium Corporation*.
8. "Charles Manson, leader of murderous cult, dead at 83". *CBS News*. New York City: CBS Corporation. November 20, 2017
9. "Transcript of Atkins's Grand Jury Testimony" Archived October 22, 2012, at the Wayback Machine, Manson Family Today.
10. Grand Jury Proceedings: Susan Denise Atkins Archived October 22, 2012, at the Wayback Machine, December 15, 1969, mansonFamilytoday.info.
11. CDCR, *History of capital punishment in California*.
12. "Susan Atkins: I'm a Political Prisoner". *TalkLeft*. May 31, 2003
13. "Judge Dismisses 'Political Prisoner' Suit" By Manson Associate. *Legal Reader*. November 30, 2003.

14. "Terminally ill Manson follower Susan Atkins dies in prison". *TheGuardian.com*.

15. "Manson's Family member Patricia Krenwinkel recommended for parole". *The Guardian*. Reuters.

16. *Meares, Hadley (October 22, 2014). "The Story of the Abandoned Movie Ranch Where the Manson Family Launched Helter Skelter".*

17. Vronsky, Peter (2007). *Female Serial Killers: How and Why Women Become Monsters*. New York City: Penguin Publishing. p. 420. ISBN 978-0-425-21390-2.

18. "Parole Hearing: Patricia Krenwinkel" (Transcript). *Cielo Drive*. Corona, California. December 29, 2016.

19. "Manson follower Patricia Krenwinkel denied parole". CNN. January 21, 2011. Archived from the original on January 22, 2011

20. "Patricia Krenwinkel Granted Parole". *cielodrive.com. May 26, 2022.*

21. "CDCR Inmate Information – Krenwinkel, Patricia"

22. Juzwiak, Rich (August 7, 2014). "Manson Girl, Patricia Krenwinkel, Gives Prison Interview". *Gawker*.

23. "Mother Accepts Blame Over Linda". *United Press International*. August 24, 1970.

24. Watson, Charles (1978). "You Were Only Waiting for This Moment". *Will You Die for Me?* ISBN 0-8007-0912-8.

25. Watkins, Paul; Soledad, Guillermo (1979). *My Life with Charles Manson*. Bantam Books. ISBN 0-553-12788-8.

26. *King, Greg (2016). Sharon Tate and the Manson Murders. Open Road Media. ISBN 9781504041720.*

27. "Tacoma-Pierce County death notices for January 2023". The News Tribune. February 19, 2023

28. Sailor, Craig. "Manson Family cult member who

provided crucial murder trial testimony dies in
Tacoma". *TheNewsTribune.com.*

29. Transcript of Subsequent Parole Consideration
Hearing. State of California. Hearing September 6,
2017. Transcribed September 16, 2017

30. Weber, Christopher (July 11, 2023). *"Leslie Van Houten,
follower of cult leader Charles Manson, released from
California prison".* AP News.

31. Guinn, Jeff: *Manson: The Life and Times of Charles Manson*

32. Interview with Leslie Van Houten". *CNN.* Larry
King Weekend. February 1, 2009.

33. Linder, Douglas O. (2014). *"The Influence of the Beatles
on Charles Manson".* Famous Trials. University of
Missouri–Kansas City School of Law.

34. Jeffrey Melnick, "Keeping Faith With the Manson
Women," *The New Yorker*, August 1, 2018

35. Karlene Faith, *The Long Prison Journey of Leslie Van
Houten: Life Beyond the Cult* (Northeastern University
Press, 2001

36. California governor again rejects parole for Manson
follower Van Houten". *UPI.* June 4, 2019.

37. "Manson follower Leslie Van Houten could be freed
after court overrules Newsom". *Los Angeles Times.* May
30, 2023

38. Waters, John (August 3, 2009). "Leslie Van Houten: A
Friendship". *Huffington Post.*

39. Steve Grogan - Clem - TateMurders.com.com

40. Steve Dennis Grogan profile, cielodrive.com;

41. Manson Family – Special Report Part 4 Steve Grogan
Paroled. Youtube.com. July 23, 2006.

42. Elias, Thomas D. (April 3, 2019). "After death penalty
reprieves, multiple Manson's confront
Newsom". *Antelope Valley Press*

43. Charles Manson follower Leslie van Houten released from prison a half-century after grisly killings". *Associated Press*. July 11, 2023.

44. Times, Los Angeles (October 5, 2012). "Charles Manson's 'right-hand man' recommended for parole". *Los Angeles Times*. ISSN 0458-3035

45. George, Edward; Matera, Dary (July 16, 1999). *Taming the Beast: Charles Manson's Life Behind Bars*. Macmillan. ISBN 9780312209704.

46. Keith Rovere (April 2023). "S1E22 - Bruce Davis: Scientology, Murder, and Manson". Spotify (Podcast). *The Lighter Side of Serial Killers with Keith Rovere*

47. Sanders, Ed (April 11, 2023). *The Family*. Hachette Books. ISBN 9780306834226.

48. CDCR Today: Parole Granted for Former Manson Family Member Bruce Davis". Archived from the original

49. "Parole Hearing: Bruce Davis 2014 | Cielodrive.com"

50. *"Parole Hearing: Bruce Davis 2019 | Cielodrive.com"*.

51. Governor Denies Parole for Former Manson Family Follower". June 18, 2021.

52. (CDCR), California Department of Corrections and Rehabilitation. "State of California Inmate Locator". *inmatelocator.cdcr.ca.gov*

53. Linder, Doug (2014). *"The Charles Manson (Tate–LaBianca Murder) Trial"*. University of Missouri–Kansas City School of Law

54. "Where Are the Manson Family Members Now? Inside Their Lives Over 50 Years After Their Killing Spree". *People.com*.

55. Watson, Charles. "FAQs". *Abounding Love Ministries*.

56. Neiswender, Mary (June 13, 1971). "Tex Watson, Honor Student, Athlete: Accused Mass Killer's Profile".

57. DeLong, William (February 19, 2024). "Methodist To Murderer: How A Young Texas Boy Became Charles Manson's Right-Hand Man". *All That's Interesting*

58. "Who Is Manson Family Member Charles 'Tex' Watson?". *Oxygen*. July 24, 2019.

59. Watson, Charles (2019). *Cease to Exist* (1 ed.). Santa Monica: 12AX7 Press. pp. 69–98. ISBN 9781083079879.

60. Waxman, Olivia B. (July 26, 2019). "Why Did the Manson Family Kill Sharon Tate? Here's the Story Charles Manson Told the Last Man Who Interviewed Him". *Time magazine*. Archived

61. Watson Convicted Of Tate Murders; Faces Sanity Trial". *The New York Times*. October 13, 1971. ISSN 0362-4331

62. *"Charles 'Tex' Watson 1978 Parole Hearing Transcript". www.cielodrive.com*

63. Watson, Charles. "Will You Die For Me?". *Abounding Love Ministries*. p. 96. Archived from the original on April 5, 2007.

64. Watson Sentenced to Death For a Part in Tate Murders". *The New York Times*. October 22, 1971. ISSN 0362-4331

65. Childress, Deirdre M. (April 30, 1984). "Slain actress Sharon Tate's mother – with tears rolling..." *upi.com*

66. *"Abounding Love Podcast with Former 'Tex Watson". Official page for the Abounding Love Podcast (Podbean). Podbean*

67. Martinez, Michael; Cary, Michael (June 13, 2012). "Judge declines to reverse order giving Manson follower tapes to police". *CNN*

68. O'Neill, Tom (2019). *Chaos: Charles Manson, the CIA, and the Secret History of the Sixties*. Little, Brown. ISBN 978-0-316-47757-4.

69. Hamilton, Matt (October 16, 2021). "Manson follower Tex Watson denied parole for Tate/La Bianca killings". The Mercury News. Archived from the original on October 19, 2021

70. Anderson, Lessley. "Lucifer, Arisen". *SF Weekly*.

71. "Informal Q & A, 2017". Bobby BeauSoleil Reference Archive. February 2017

72. Breznikar, Klemen (July 27, 2014). "Bobby BeauSoleil interview (The Orkustra)". *It's Psychedelic Baby! Magazine*.

73. "Bobby Beausoleil". *Biography.com*. A&E Television Networks.

74. Sederstrom, Jill (September 18, 2018). "The Story Behind The Murder That Set Off The Manson Family". *Oxygen*.

75. Yuko, Elizabeth (January 4, 2019). "Manson Family Associate Bobby Beausoleil Recommended for Parole". *Rolling Stone*.

76. Associated Press, "Manson's Pal Found Guilty Of Murder," *The San Bernardino Sun-Telegram*, San Bernardino, California, Sunday, April 19, 1970,

77. Sobel, Barbara (April 30, 2019). "Bobby Beausoleil, Manson Family Member, Parole Reversed by Governor". *Guardian Liberty Voice*.

78. Peter Levenda (June 1, 2011). *Sinister Forces—The Manson Secret: A Grimoire of American Political Witchcraft*. Trine Day. ISBN 978-0984185832.

79. "The Farcical Capote Interview". *Bobby BeauSoleil Reference Archive*. December 2016.

80. Keefe, Patrick Radden (March 22, 2013). "Truman Capote's Co-Conspirators". *Newyorker.com*.

81. Gary Hinman | Charles Manson Family and Sharon Tate-Labianca Murders | Cielodrive.com

82. Gary Hinman's Family Reacts to Charles Manson's Death

83. What were the events that led up to the Tate murders? | Britannica

84. Bobby Beausoleil and the Last Manson Mystery

85. Peterson, Bettelou (August 14, 1969). *Jay Sebring, Man with a Successful Idea*. Detroit Free Press.

86. White, Carrie (2011). *Upper Cut: Highlights of My Hollywood Life*. Atria Books ISBN 9781439199091.

87. Tannen, Mary (August 18, 2002). "Message In A Shampoo Bottle". *The New York Times*.

88. Would you pay $50 for a haircut?". *Star-News*. August 3, 1963

89. Manson Victim's Friend Posits Alternative Motive: "I Never Bought into the Race War Theory"". *The Hollywood Reporter*.

90. Jay Sebring Documentary Lands at Shout! Studios (Exclusive). *The Hollywood Reporter*. February 26, 2020.

91. "*Jay Sebring Is the Godfather of Men's Hairstyling. So Why Haven't You Heard of Him?*". Esquire. October 1, 2020.

92. "Remembering Jay Sebring, Hollywood's First Celebrity Hairstylist". *Vogue*. September 22, 2020

93. Tate–LaBianca murders - Wikipedia

94. Frykowski, Wojciech | friend of Polanski | Britannica

95. Wojciech Frykowski - Helter Skelter - CharlesManson.com

96. Abigail Folger | Ultimate Pop Culture Wiki | Fandom

97. Romano, Aja (August 7, 2019). *The Manson Family murders, and their complicated legacy, explained*.

98. "Sharon Tate Autopsy"

99. Bishari, Nuala Sawyer (July 9, 2018) [July 9, 2018]. "Yesterday's Crimes: The Helter Skelter Heiress". *SFWeekly*

100. California Abolishes Death Penalty". *The Journal (Ogdensburg, N.Y.)*. AP. February 18, 1972.

101. Woo, Elaine (September 26, 2009). "Susan Atkins dies at 61; imprisoned Charles Manson follower". *Los Angeles Times*.

102. "Donald 'Shorty' Shea". *www.cielodrive.com*

103. Montaldo, Charles (3 July 2019). "Manson Family Murder Victim Donald 'Shorty' Shea's Revenge". *ThoughtCo.*

104. Steven Parent | Tate murders victim | Britannica

105. Petruzzello, Melissa. "Sharon Tate". *Encyclopedia Britannica*.

106. Sandford, C. (2009). *Polanski: A Biography*. St. Martin's Press. ISBN 978-0-230-61176-

107. Paul Tate, 82; Investigated Murder of Daughter Sharon Tate". *Los Angeles Times*. May 24, 2005

108. Kraemer, Kristin (July 26, 2019). "A cult murdered this Richland beauty queen. Sharon Tate is featured in a new Hollywood film". *Tri-City Herald*

109. Sanders, Ed (2002). *The Family*. Thunder's Mouth Press. ISBN 1-56025-396-7.

110. Hughes, David (August 14, 2019). "Sharon Tate murder: the true story of the actress portrayed in Once Upon a Time in Hollywood, killed by the Manson Family". *The i Paper*.

111. Dunne, Dominick (1999). *The Way We Lived Then: Recollections of a Well-Known Name Dropper*. Crown Publishers. ISBN 0-609-60388-4.

112. "The Story of the Tate Family". Tate Family Legacy website

113. How a Music Producer Was Tied to Charles Manson — and Possibly Evaded His Murder". *Oxygen*. November 15, 2024

114.   Vulliamy, Ed; Vulliamy, By Ed (March 7, 1999). "Manson set to defend himself, 30 years on". *The Guardian*. ISSN 0261-3077.

115.   "Long Before Little Charlie Became the Face of Evil". *The New York Times*. August 7, 2013

116.   Lansing, H. Allegra (July 11, 2019). "Son of Man: The Early Life of Charles Manson". *Medium*. Boston, Massachusetts: A Medium Corporation

117.   Maslin, Janet (August 6, 2013). "Long Before Little Charlie Became the Face of Evil". *The New York Times*. New York City

118.   Charles Manson – Diane Sawyer Documentary.

119.   Smith, David E; Luce, John (1971). *Love Needs Care: A History of San Francisco's Haight-Ashbury Free Medical Clinic and Its Pioneer Role Treating Drug-abuse Problems*. Boston, Little, Brown.

120.   Melnick, Jeffrey Paul (2018). *Creepy Crawling: Charles Manson and the Many Lives of America's Most Infamous Family*. Arcade. ISBN 978 1628728934.

121.   Emmons, Nuel (1988). *Manson in His Own Words*. Grove Press. ISBN 0-8021-3024-0.

122.   Bitette, Nicole (August 31, 2016). "Beach Boy Mike Love alleges bandmate watched Charles Manson carry out murder". *New York Daily News*.

123.   Gill, Lauren (November 16, 2017). "Remember, Charles Manson Was a White Supremacist". *Newsweek*

124.   Thompson, Desire (November 20, 2017). "Charles Manson & His Obsession with Black People". *Vibe*. New York City

125.   Whitehead, John W. (August 3, 2010). "Helter Skelter: Racism and Murder". *HuffPost*.

126.   Beckerman, Jim (August 9, 2019). "Charles Manson: 50 years later, murders have a racist link to recent mass-killings". *The Record*.

127. Waxman, Olivia B. (July 26, 2019). "Why Did the Manson Family Kill Sharon Tate? Here's the Story Charles Manson Told the Last Man Who Interviewed Him". *Time magazine.*

128. Did The Manson Family Have Other Victims?". *CBS News.* March 16, 2008.

129. Romano, Aja (August 7, 2019). "The Manson Family murders, and their complicated legacy, explained". *Vox.*

130. Pelisek, Christine (February 22, 2019). "Did Charles Manson Have 4 More Victims? 'There's an Answer There Somewhere,' Says LAPD Detective". *People.*

131. "Would-Be Assassin 'Squeaky' Fromme Released from Prison". *ABC.* August 14, 2009.

132. "Manson moved to a tougher prison after a drug charge". *Sun Journal.* Lewiston, Maine. AP. August 22, 1997

133. Hedegaard, Erik (November 21, 2013). "Charles Manson Today: The Final Confessions of a Psychopath". *Rolling Stone.*

134. Charles Manson Dead at 83". *Rolling Stone.*

135. Dillon, Nancy (November 24, 2017). "Battle erupts over control of Charles Manson's remains, estate". *New York Daily News.*

136. Feldman, Kate (November 28, 2017). "Charles Manson's secret prison pen pal Michael Channels wants murderer's body". *New York Daily News.*

137. "Charles Manson: The Incredible Story of the Most Dangerous Man Alive". *Rolling Stone.* August 8, 2017

138. Lusher, Adam (November 20, 2017). "Charles Manson: Neo-Nazis hail serial killer a visionary and try to resurrect fascist movement created on his orders". *The Independent.* London, United Kingdom.

139. Dennis Wilson interview Archived December 15,

2007, at the Wayback Machine *Circus* magazine, October 26, 1976.

140. "Charles Manson Issues Album Under Creative Commons - News and Analysis by PC Magazine". July 10, 2009.

141. "Watch This Chilling Manson Documentary from 1973". *vice.com*. Vice. November 20, 2017

142. Stebbins, Jon (2000). *Dennis Wilson: The Real Beach Boy*. ECW Press. ISBN 978-1-55022-404-7.

143. Bugliosi, Vincent; Gentry, Curt (1974). *Helter Skelter: The True Story of the Manson Murders* (1992 ed.). Norton. ISBN 0-09-997500-9.

144. Udo, Tommy (2002). *Charles Manson: Music, Mayhem, Murder*. Sanctuary Records. ISBN 1-86074-388-9.

145. LeBlanc, Jerry; Davis, Ivor (1971). *5 to Die*. Holloway House Publishing. ISBN 0-87067-306-8.

146. Gilmore, John (2000). *Manson: The Unholy Trail of Charlie and the Family*. Amok Books. ISBN 1-878923-13-7.

147. 'Then It All Came Down': Truman Capote Interviews Bobby Beausoleil. San Quentin, 1973. | Truman Capote

148. Obituaries: Terry Melcher. *The Daily Telegraph*. November 23, 2004.

149. Oliver, Myrna (November 22, 2004). "Terry Melcher helped create the surf music sound". *Los Angeles Times*.

150. Rogan, Johnny (1998). *The Byrds: Timeless Flight Revisited* (2nd ed.). Rogan House. ISBN 978-0-9529-5401-9.

151. Cozzen, R. Duane (August 11, 2015). *BRUCE & TERRY, Bruce Johnston & Terry Melcher, Singles (45's)*. Surf & Hot Rod Music of the '60s ISBN 978-1-3294-0033-7.

152. Paul Werner, *Polański. Biografia*, Poznań: Rebis, 2013

153. Berendt, Joanna (6 December 2016). "Roman Polanski

Extradition Request Rejected by Poland's Supreme Court". *The New York Times*.

154. Polanski, Roman; Bernstein, Catherine (5 May 2006). "*Mémoires de la Shoah: témoignage de Roman Polanski, enfant de déporté, enfant caché, né le 18 août 1933*"

155. "Sharon Tate's Family bares 'Restless Souls'" Archived 25 June 2012 at the Wayback Machine, *USA Today*.

156. Bradshaw, Peter (15 July 2005). "profile: Roman Polanski, The Guardian, Guardian Unlimited". *The Guardian*. London

157. "Roman Polanski, UXL Newsmakers, Find Articles at BNET.com". Findarticles.com

158. "Biography". Movies.yahoo.com 2009

159. Cronin, Paul (2005). *Roman Polanski: Interviews*. University Press of Mississippi. ISBN 1578067995.

160. Polański, Roman (1984). *Roman*. Morrow (ibidem). p. 73. ISBN 0688026214.

161. Glazer, Mitchell. *Rolling Stone* magazine, 2 April 1981

162. "Polanski Seeks Sex Case Dismissal – 3 December 2008". Thesmokinggun.com.

163. Ain-Krupa, Julia, Roman Polanski: A Life in Exile, ABC Clio, Santa Barbara, California, 2010

164. Sandford, Christopher, Polanski: A Biography, 2008, Palgrave Macmillan

165. Romney, Jonathan (5 October 2008). "Roman Polanski: The truth about his notorious sex crime". *The Independent*. London

166. "Timeline of Director Roman Polanski's Life". *The Washington Post*. Associated Press. 28 September 2009.

167. "Roman Polanski First Interview After Arrest – Diane Sawyer – video Dailymotion"

168. "Alleged victim defends Polanski and criticises 'opportunistic' protesters". *Irish News*. 8 April 2020

169. "Polanski charged with rape". *Eugene Register-Guard*. (Oregon). UPI. 13 March 1977.

170. "Polanski Pleads Not Guilty in Drug-Rape Case". *Los Angeles Times*. 16 April 1977

171. Romney, Jonathan (5 October 2008). "Roman Polanski: The truth about his notorious sex crime". *The Independent*. UK

172. "Polanski ducks out on court". *Spokesman-Review*. (Spokane, Washington). Associated Press. 2 February 1978

173. "Polanski in Paris; extradition unlikely". *Eugene Register-Guard*. Associated Press. 2 February 1978

174. Polanski Victim Blames Media" Archived 4 March 2016 at the Wayback Machine ABC News video, 10 March 2011

175. Smith, Dave (January 26, 1971). "Mother Tells Life of Manson as Boy". *Los Angeles Times*.

176. Lansing, H. Allegra (July 11, 2019). "Son of Man: The Early Life of Charles Manson". *Medium*. Boston, Massachusetts: A Medium Corporation

177. Maslin, Janet (August 6, 2013). "Long Before Little Charlie Became the Face of Evil". *The New York Times*. New York City.

178. Smith, David E; Luce, John (1971). *Love Needs Care: A History of San Francisco's Haight-Ashbury Free Medical Clinic and Its Pioneer Role Treating Drug-abuse Problems*. Boston, Little, Brown

179. Roberts, Steven V. (December 7, 1969). "Charlie Manson, Nomadic Guru, Flirted With Crime in a Turbulent Childhood". *The New York Times*. p. 84.

180. Nolan, Tom (November 11, 1971). "Beach Boys: A California Saga, Part II". *Rolling Stone*.

About the Author

Alan R Warren is a Bestselling Author, Producer, and host of the popular NBC Radioshow *House of Mystery* and *Inside Writing*, both heard on the 106.5 F.M. Los Angeles/102.3 F.M. Riverside/ 1050 A.M. Palm Springs/ 540 A.M. KYAH Salt Lake City/ 1150 A.M. KKNW Seattle/Tacoma and Phoenix.

His bestselling true crime books in Canada include *Beyond Suspicion: The True Story of Colonel Russell Williams*, which will be featured on CNN's *Lies, Crimes, & Videos* (Season 4), and *Murder Times Six: The True Story of the Wells Gray Park Murders*. In America, his bestsellers include *The Killing Game: Serial Killer Rodney Alcala*, which was featured on several television shows such as *Very Scary People with Donny Walberg*, Oxygen's *Mark of a Killer*, Reelz' *Killer Trophies*, and soon to be included in a four-part Sundance Channel documentary called *Death's Date*. His bestseller, *Doomsday Cults: The Devil's Hostages*, was featured on Vice's *Dark Side of the '90s*.

His latest series, *Killer Queens*, is a six-part book series covering murders that affect the Gay Community. So far, it includes Book 1 - Leopold & Loeb, Book 2 - Butcher of Hanover: Fritz Haarmann, Book 3 - Grindr Serial Killer: Stephen Port, and Book 4 - Bruce McArthur: Toronto Gay Killer.

Also in The House of Mystery Interviews Series

The *House of Mystery Radio Show* has been on the air for ten years, broadcasting in over a dozen cities in the U.S. It started as a way to interview guests knowledgeable in many of the world's mysteries involving crime, science, religion, history, paranormal, conspiracies, etc. The *House of Mystery Interviews Series* is a curated collection of interviews from the show. Each volume focuses on one of the mysteries, providing the background and reproducing the main points discussed in the interviews. There will be no committed answer at the end, as the Interviews series does not attempt to solve the case. Instead, it provides the most compelling aspects of each theory held by different experts. This series is an excellent reference for researchers and a good overview for those unfamiliar with the case. Online links to the actual interviews are included.

VOLUME 1: JACK THE RIPPER: THE INTERVIEWS

Volume 1 of the Interview Series, "Jack the Ripper," covers the ultimate "who-done-it" mystery of 1888 London. Scotland Yard's "Whitechapel Murder File," in which Jack the Ripper had a starring role, went cold before it could be solved. One hundred thirty-two years later, the fascination with this cold case mystery continues. Ripperologists passionately debate suspects, opinions, research methods, and theories. Even which murder victims to include in the case is widely debated. Astonishingly, work continues, and today Ripperologists still find new clues that bring us closer to solving the mystery.

the HOUSE OF MYSTERY RADIOSHOW presents

JACK *the* RIPPER

THE INTERVIEWS: VOLUME 1

ALAN R. WARREN
MICHAEL L. HAWLEY

The mix of credible and diverse thinkers interviewed includes world-renowned historian Neil Storey, the Godfather of Ripper Research, Paul Begg, Ripperologists: Paul Williams, Tom Wescott, Adam Wood, and Steve Blomer. Michael Hawley contributes his unprecedented scientific approach to the case. Suspect Ripperologists Jeff Mudgett, whose great-great-grandfather was serial killer H.H. Holmes, weighs in, as does Russell Edwards, who believes he solved the mystery through DNA.

VOLUME 2: JFK ASSASSINATION: THE INTERVIEWS

Volume 2 of the Interview Series, "JFK Assassination," covers *the* unrivaled historical mystery of historical mysteries. The JFK assassination is the grandfather of all conspiracies in America and arguably where they all started. A highly popular President with movie star looks and charisma, effecting significant changes in society, was brutally cut down in his prime. The official story was that

the HOUSE OF MYSTERY RADIOSHOW presents

JFK ASSASSINATION

THE INTERVIEWS: VOLUME 2

ALAN R. WARREN

Foreword by VINCENT PALAMARA

JFK was killed by a lone assassin, Lee Harvey Oswald. However, many conspiracy theorists believe in an assassination plot involving the FBI, CIA, U.S. military, VP LBJ, Cuba's Fidel Castro, Russia's KGB, the Mafia, or some combination of those entities.

The research and interviewing of the JFK assassination experts lasted for over six years. Arguments and counter-arguments from a diverse mix of bestselling authors make for some interesting discussions. And some of the authors interviewed are considered just as controversial as the mystery itself. Most authors focused on who they believed was responsible for the assassination. Others narrowed their focus on certain related aspects, such as the Zapruder film, the Nix film, the Garrison Tapes, etc. All information collected from each expert adds value to the overall mystery.

VOLUME 3: ZODIAC KILLER: THE INTERVIEWS

Volume 3 of the Interview Series, "Zodiac Killer," covers another serial killer who has stayed in the spotlight for years after their case went cold. It's been over 40 years now, and fascination with the Zodiac is still going strong. Experts passionately debate Zodiac suspects, Zodiac's letters/ciphers, opinions, and theories. Even which murder victims to include in the case is widely debated.

The diverse mix of authors interviewed includes cryptologist and cipher expert David Oranchak, authors who propose their suspects are already convicted serial killers, authors who claim the Zodiac was their father, authors who offer new or already considered suspects, and an author who argues the Zodiac killer didn't exist at all and that Zodiac was a hoax.

VOLUME 4: MYSTERIOUS CELEBRITY DEATHS: THE INTERVIEWS

Volume 4 of the Interview Series, "Mysterious Celebrity Deaths," covers interviews relating to the mysterious deaths of the influential rock band Nirvana's frontman Kurt Cobain, the 1960s mega-icon Marilyn Monroe, T.V.'s *Hogan's Heroes* lead actor Bob Crane, the talented and multi-award-winning actress Natalie Wood, and the people's princess, Princess Diana.

the HOUSE OF MYSTERY
RADIOSHOW presents

MYSTERIOUS CELEBRITY DEATHS

THE INTERVIEWS: VOLUME 4

ALAN R. WARREN
Foreword by ERIC SHAPIRO

VOLUME 5: CONSPIRACY THEORY CULTURE: THE INTERVIEWS

Volume 5 of the *House of Mystery Interviews Series* will focus on theories that go against the scientific facts that we have learned over many generations of the human race. There is something uniquely intriguing about a good conspiracy theory. They tell tales of heroes, villains, and alternative realities. Conspiracy theories represent secret knowledge: real or not,

the HOUSE OF MYSTERY
RADIOSHOW presents

CONSPIRACY THEORY CULTURE

THE INTERVIEWS: VOLUME 5

ALAN R. WARREN
Foreword by Dr. JOSEPH USCINSKI

and there is something very pleasing about having supposed insider knowledge.

Because of their entertainment value, you can find conspiracy theories everywhere. Implausibility doesn't make conspiracy theories less entertaining. What if the moon landing was faked? Who would have been involved? How could they have pulled it off, and why? What if the Earth is encapsulated by a celestial lid? What if the infamous leader of the Third Reich escaped Germany? What if President Franklin Roosevelt had allowed the Pearl Harbor attacks to happen?

These are a few of the conspiracy theories discussed in this volume. As with the others in this series, this book will cover the most popular conspiracies – the ones that have gained lots of ground in the media and on the internet. Some of them even have celebrity followers. During the interviews, guests were shown the utmost respect, as we tried to find out their reasoning for believing what they do and how they developed their beliefs.

VOLUME 6: PARANORMAL & THE OCCULT: THE INTERVIEWS

Volume 6 of the *House of Mystery Interviews Series* covers the fields of the Paranormal and the Occult. During the first 10 years of the show, the paranormal field was very popular in society, including several television' series on air covering the hunt for ghosts, haunted houses, mediums communicating with the dead, witchcraft, and

the HOUSE OF MYSTERY RADIOSHOW presents

PARANORMAL & THE OCCULT

THE INTERVIEWS: VOLUME 6

ALAN R. WARREN

even Satanism or spirituality, as religion quite often is given the power to wither protect or attack one doing the investigation.

Each interview selected for this book was chosen for the guest's believability in the area of their expertise in the paranormal field. The book is divided into several sections covering mediums, Parapsychology, Occult influences such as the Church of Satan and Witches, and the tools used, like an Ouija Board, Tarot, Astrology, and Numerology.

Mediums & Psychics:

David Wells explains Past Life Regression & Qabalah, while Derek Acorah talks about his Spiritualist Mediumship in TV's *Ghost Town*. Rob Gutro communicates with your pets in the afterlife, and Gary Mannion does Psychic Surgery to heal people. Mark Allan Frost channels a spirit named Seth, and James Van Praagh shows us Survival Mediumship Evidence.

Paranormal Tools:

Robert Murch details talking boards, including the Ouija board, while Michael M. Hughes gives the history of the Tarot & its many uses. Johnny Zaffis collects haunted dolls and more for his museum. Steven Frampton successfully uses Astrology to help people become successful in business, and Alison Baughman uses Numerology to make lives better.

Religions & Occult:

Magus Peter Gilmore runs the Church of Satan, while Winter Laake describes what Luciferian life is like. Jeffrey Seelman clears houses of dark spirits and performs exorcisms, and Krystal Madison is the "Witch from Sleepy Hollow."

Mind Over Matter:

Robert Waggoner has been Lucid Dreaming for over 30 years now, and Lyn Buchanan learned Controlled Remote Viewing while serving in the Military. Uri Geller uses psychokinesis to bend spoons with his mind, and Diane Corcoran has monitored Near-Death Experiences for over 30 years.

Parapsychology:

Dr. Ciaran O'Keefe from TV's *Most Haunted*, Steve Parsons from ParaScience, and Lloyd Auerbach aka "Professor Paranormal," discuss Parapsychology.

VOLUME 7: D.B. COOPER

Volume 7 reviews the D.B. Cooper case. It is divided into five parts. The first part gives the bare facts we know about the hijacking. The second part covers the primary suspects listed according to the FBI, media, or public opinion, supported by the show's best interviews with authors and researchers who covered these suspects. The

third part covers the other major suspects popular among the public but not considered Cooper by the FBI or law enforcement authorities. The fourth part covers some of the major suspects who came forward to police and confessed to being D.B. Cooper. The last part is dedicated to the wave of copycat hijackings that occurred after the Cooper case. And there were quite a few.

www.ingramcontent.com/pod-product-compliance
Lightning Source LLC
Chambersburg PA
CBHW070859120626
46546CB00001B/66